The Fear of Population Decline

The Fear of Population Decline

MICHAEL S. TEITELBAUM
Alfred P. Sloan Foundation
New York, New York

JAY M. WINTER
Pembroke College
University of Cambridge
Cambridge, England

1985

ACADEMIC PRESS, INC.
Harcourt Brace Jovanovich, Publishers
Orlando   San Diego   New York   Austin
London   Montreal   Sydney   Tokyo   Toronto

HB
871
.T33
1985

ACADEMIC PRESS, INC.
Orlando, Florida 32887

United Kingdom Edition published by
ACADEMIC PRESS INC. (LONDON) LTD.
24–28 Oval Road, London NW1 7DX

LIBRARY OF CONGRESS CATALOGING IN PUBLICATION DATA

Teitelbaum, Michael S.
    The fear of population decline.

    Includes index.
    1. Population.   2. Population policy.   I. Winter, J. M.
II. Title.   III. Title: Population decline.
HB871.T33   1985   304.6'2   85-3930
ISBN 0-12-685190-5 (alk. paper)
ISBN 0-12-685191-3 (paperback)

PRINTED IN THE UNITED STATES OF AMERICA

85 86 87 88   9 8 7 6 5 4 3 2 1

Contents

CONTENTS

CONTENTS

List of Tables and Figures

Tables

Figures

LIST OF TABLES AND FIGURES

Preface

A vast literature exists on the subject of population growth, but relatively little informed discussion is available on the subject of population decline. Partly, this is due to the fact that the field of demography developed most rapidly in the post–Second World War period, when the baby boom was in full swing and when attention was directed appropriately toward rapid population growth in the developing world. Patterns of declining mortality and sustained high fertility became major foci of both historical and contemporary demographic research.

Since about 1965, when the baby boom turned into the baby bust in most Western countries, and when total fertility rates fell below the notional replacement level of 2.1 children per woman, the oddity of slow population growth, no growth at all, or even decline (negative growth) began to attract more and more comment. Some of this contemporary discussion has been even-tempered; other expressions vary from the emotional to the hysterical. It seemed wise, therefore, to try to provide a dispassionate survey of a subject which is potentially explosive in political terms.

In this effort, our aim has been to broaden the discussion of recent population issues. Most quantitative studies acknowledge the importance of cultural and political forces in the evolution of trends and policies, but few have attempted to give equal weight to both the statistical and ideological evidence pertaining to these questions. Similarly, nonquantitative discussions focus upon cultural and political attitudes and perceptions but often lack a rigorous demographic framework against which to measure contemporary comment. Even in the few notable cases where a more comprehensive approach is adopted, such as in the work of the economist J. J. Spengler, the study of opinion on population issues is restricted to the writings of economists or politicians. We felt it appropriate to go further and to try to locate the phenomenon of population decline in both the wider cultural history and the demographic history of Europe and the United States over the past century.

The structure of the book is designed to show the extent to which current demographic developments form a part of a much longer continuum of discussion and behavior. In the first chapter we outline some of the confusions which plague the subject of population decline, and then proceed in Chapters 2 and 3 to demonstrate the complex ways in which fears of population decline emerged in the period 1870–1940. In Chapter 4, we describe developments in the period 1945–1965, when these fears temporarily receded. The phenomenon of the so-called baby bust and policy responses to it are discussed in Chapters 5 and 6. In the final chapter, we summarize the long debate over the nature and possible dangers of population decline, and then turn to the question of likely demographic trends, and what to do about them, in the foreseeable future.

The phenomena and perceptions addressed in this study are likely to affect the lives of most of us in the near future. We therefore have sought to couch our discussion of what inevitably are technical questions in terms that are accessible to people of varying interests and backgrounds. The views expressed here are those of the authors and not of their respective institutions.

Many people have given generously of their time and advice in the course of the preparation of this book. In particular, we thank E. A. Wrigley and V. R. Berghahn for critical comments and L. F. Bouvier, C. E. Davis, G. Calot, and C. Blayo for permission to reproduce data. Of course, the authors accept responsibility for all evidence and interpretations presented; and for any errors that still remain, each author blames the other.

The Nature of
Population Decline

THE RECURRENT FEAR OF POPULATION DECLINE

After a generation of debate about population growth, it may seem perverse or idiosyncratic to raise the subject of population decline. However, as this book will show, the discussion of population decline has a long and—to judge by the prominence of many who worried about it—a distinguished history of its own.

That history has never been fully explored. To do so is to see how demographic issues have touched the most important political and social questions of the past century, both in Europe and in North America. This is not to say that anxiety about population decline has been constant over the past 100 years. It ebbs and flows, depending both upon demographic realities and perceptions of the links between population change and economic, social, and political power.

In the West the fear of population decline last flourished during the Great Depression of the interwar years. It went into remission during the two postwar decades from 1945 to the mid-1960s. Since that time, anxious voices have been raised again, first in the socialist states of Eastern Europe, then in Western Europe, and most recently in North America.

These cries of alarm are less shrill than those of the 1930s, but there are unmistakable signs that concern about population decline is on the rise. Indeed, in some countries pronatalist policy measures verging on the draconian have been proposed or enacted, and the whole subject is further complicated by the fact that demographic trends in the developed and the developing world have diverged to an unprecedented degree.

It may therefore be of some importance today to reflect on the modern history of concern about population decline. The debates we shall describe, both past and present, are permeated with confusions and misunderstandings that warrant discussion and clarification. The relevant data require both elaboration and interpretation. The ideologies that underlie many perceptions need exposition and assessment. Furthermore, whether those concerned like it or not, slow growth (or even slow decline) is likely to characterize Western population change in the near future. To escape from the expectations and perceptions of a past of relatively rapid population growth is, therefore, a vital prerequisite of informed discussion of population questions today. It is to help in this adjustment of perspective that this book has been written.

IMAGES AND TERMINOLOGIES

Discussions of population decline have almost always conjured up a multitude of alarming images. Many of them have revealed fears not only about numbers but also about the quality, vitality, or optimistic outlook of a nation's inhabitants. The interchangeable and overlapping nature of quantitative and qualitative statements inevitably adds elements of confusion and emotion to many reflections on this subject. In some cases there is clearly a presumption that the phenomenon of "decline" leads naturally to "fall," a notion which may be derived from a cursory reading of much Western literature, from Gibbon to Spengler to Evelyn Waugh.

In France, where public debate on the question has been reverberating for at least a century, histrionic rhetoric abounds. Some of it is voiced by extremists or fringe elements; but much else pours from the pens of distinguished and well-known public figures. For instance, in 1979, Michel Jobert, formerly foreign minister under de Gaulle, contributed an article entitled *"Comment un pays meurt"* ("How a Nation Dies") to a collection of essays by prominent academics and writers entitled *La France ridée* ("Withered France"). More recently, Jacques Chirac, the conservative former prime minister who is currently mayor of Paris and prospective presidential candidate of the Gaullist *Rassemblement pour la République* (RPR), described the current demographic situation of France as "terrifying" and Europe as "vanishing." (For a fuller description of

Chirac's statement, see Chapter 6.) In the pages of newspapers with outlooks as diverse as *Le Monde* and *Figaro*, respected writers in the past few years have raised the specters of autogenocide, collective suicide, or the demographic menace of population decline (as cited in Huss, 1980).

Even French terminology reflects this orientation. The term in French for a decline in the birth rate is *dénatalité*, which carries a much stronger (and more negative) emphasis than its English equivalent. Frequently, indictment takes the place of analysis. To write of "demographic bankruptcy" or *The Refusal of Life*, in the historian Pierre Chaunu's (1975) phrase, is to accuse couples of personal failure, selfishness, and inhumanity if they choose to have small families.

Such strong terminology is not limited to France. A report on a 1984 meeting of experts convened in Montreal by the Canadian government described population increase as "one of the major factors contributing toward a dynamic society." It noted the high cost of pronatalist incentives, but went on to question

> whether the goal of maintaining the population was not as important as that of national defence. Perhaps as much could be spent for the first as for the second; in the long term, there is no point in "defending" a population that is disappearing! (Canada, 1984a, pp. 5, 8)

If some writers continue to see how fertility decline "causes" a nation's decline, others have reversed the argument in order to assert that low fertility is a clear sign that a nation is in decline or in turmoil. The notion of fertility decline as a symptom rather than the cause of social decline is an old one, as we shall see later, but among its most distinguished recent exponents is Alexander Solzhenitsyn. In an article in *The Times* (London) of 11 May 1982, he lamented the demise of Russian culture, which, he believes, received a mortal wound under Communism. After posing the question "Will it ever rise again?" he turned immediately to demography. "As to the Russian people," he noted,

> as demonstrated by Western demographers, it has moved into a phase of biological degeneracy. Within a century or perhaps even sooner, it will be diminished by one-half and dissolve itself and almost vanish from the face of the earth. And this development appears irreversible. (p. 12)

I. THE NATURE OF POPULATION DECLINE

It may be true that the impulse toward conjuring up such over-dramatized images is a strong one and has been so for generations, but it is certainly not immutable. The first step in separating emotive from analytical statements is to clarify the meaning of some of the key terms used in the discussion of population change.

THE DEMOGRAPHY OF POPULATION DECLINE

The concepts surrounding population decline appear simple only to those who do not appreciate the complexities of demographic measurement and projection. A year-to-year decline in the birth rate often is taken to mean that women are producing smaller families, which may or may not be the case. A demographic projection incorporating low-fertility assumptions frequently is taken as a prediction that population size is heading for decline, a flagrant misinterpretation of the meaning of demographic projection. Such misuse of demography may be either benign or malevolent in intent, but the misinforming effect is the same.

Hence a clear understanding of the relevant concepts of demography is a necessity before any sensible discussion of the fear of population decline can be initiated. Some of the concepts and relationships are simple and straightforward; others are subtle and often counterintuitive. All deserve brief elaboration here.

The Basic Population Equation

Human populations can grow or decline by virtue of the combined impacts of four separable forces: births, deaths, in-migration, and out-migration. (For the world population as a whole, the latter two can presumably be ignored, barring large-scale interplanetary movements.) This gives rise to a simple equation that ought to be kept in mind in all discussions of population decline:

$$\text{Population at time } y = \text{population at time } x$$
$$+ \text{ births from time } x \text{ to time } y$$
$$- \text{ deaths from time } x \text{ to time } y$$
$$+ \text{ in-migrants from time } x \text{ to time } y$$
$$- \text{ out-migrants from time } x \text{ to time } y$$

4

This simple equation demonstrates that we must know something of births, deaths, and net immigration before we can assess the growth or decline of a national population. While this may appear self-evident, it is surprising how often one finds discussions of population trends that report on fertility declines but fail to take account of trends in mortality or net immigration.

Measurements of Fertility, Mortality, and Growth

The basic population equation gives us only a first approximation of underlying demographic rates because it is obvious that the number of births, deaths, and net migrants must be related to some denominator if they are to be comprehensible. Otherwise a large, slow-growing population might be incorrectly seen as growing faster than a small, rapidly growing population. The choice of denominator, however, determines the meaning of the calculated rate, and not infrequently the uninitiated misinterpret the meaning of the various rates available.

The simplest and most widely used rates are so-called *crude rates*, in which the denominator is simply the size of the population that produces the stated number of births, deaths, or net migrants. (More precisely, the denominator of a crude rate is the person-years lived in the time interval—typically a calendar year—often represented as the average population size over the interval.) Such rates are by convention expressed per 1000 population, thus yielding a so-called *birth rate* of, for example, 15 per 1000 or a *death rate* of 10 per 1000. The difference between the crude birth rate and the crude death rate is termed the *crude rate of natural increase*, which in the above example would be 15 − 10, or 5 per 1000 (or 0.5%). In-migration and out-migration can be incorporated in the same manner, thereby yielding crude rates of population growth (i.e., natural increase as modified by net migration).

Crude rates are very useful for some purposes, but quite misleading for others. They are, of course, heavily influenced by the age structure (that is, the proportions in each age group) of the population producing them. To illustrate with an extreme example, imagine a population with no one under age 50. Such a population would have a very high crude death rate and a very low (perhaps 0) crude birth rate. But the mortality and fertility rates for the existing age groups might be identical to those over age 50 in a more normal population whose overall crude death rate and birth rate would reflect the different mortality and fertility schedules of the population under age 50.

In the real world, population age structures do differ substantially, albeit not to the extreme degree of the above example. As a result, comparisons of crude rates across populations, or over time for the same population, must be done in a manner that adjusts for differences in age structure. This need gives rise to *age-adjusted rates*, in which the events of birth or death are ascribed to those population age groups at risk of experiencing them. Hence the *general fertility rate* divides the number of births by the number of women of reproductive age, and the *total fertility rate* is a composite of all the age-specific rates for each age group (e.g., births to women aged 20–24 ÷ women aged 20–24) within the reproductive life span. For mortality, the analogues are the age-specific rates that form components of the life table, (i.e., life expectation at age x, etc.). A life table describes the mortality schedule of a closed (nonmigrating) population in a form enabling us to state the probability that a person will die at any given age.

Ultimately these rates give rise to combined fertility–mortality measures that incorporate adjustments for differences in age structure. These include the *net reproduction rate* and the *intrinsic rate of natural increase* derived from it. Both reflect the tendency of the population to increase or decline, net of the effects of age structure. Neither encompasses the effects of in- and out-migration.

From the net reproduction rate comes the concept of *replacement fertility*. Simply stated, replacement fertility occurs when the fertility of a given generation of women is exactly sufficient to replace itself with a new generation of women equal in size, taking account of the mortality expected under prevailing mortality conditions. (Put another way, replacement fertility occurs when the net reproduction rate equals 1.) In low-mortality societies, replacement fertility requires approximately 2.1 children per woman, to allow for the fact that a small number of girl babies die before reproductive age, and also that somewhat more than half of births are male and hence excludable from the net reproduction calculation.

The intrinsic rate of natural increase is the underlying growth rate once the effects of age structure have been controlled for. It differs from the crude rate of natural increase in that the latter can be heavily affected by age structure. The importance of this distinction for understanding contemporary trends has never been greater, because at present fertility levels in many of the nations of the industrialized world are below replacement levels, and hence the intrinsic rates of natural increase are negative. At the same time, the age structures of most industrial countries still reflect the relatively high fertility levels of the two postwar decades (see Chapter 4), and hence the crude rates of natural increase tend to still be positive.

Both the intrinsic and crude rates are meaningful and important, but they tell us different things. In fact, much of the confusion afflicting discussions of population decline results from confusion about these crude and intrinsic concepts.

How a Population Ages

The demographic causes of the aging of populations are quite counterintuitive. Common sense tells us that societies age with declining mortality and increasing longevity, that is, people live longer so there are relatively more old people.

The reality is otherwise—typically populations age following declining *fertility,* rather than mortality. This is true because mortality improvements generally operate at all ages. Effective immunity against the type of cancer and cardiovascular disease prevalent among the elderly might be partial exceptions, though such medical advances would probably also prove useful for other age groups. Meanwhile, fertility changes affect the numbers of only one age group—the very young, or specifically those aged 0. Two minor caveats here are that in countries with very high maternal mortality, fertility declines would also reduce mortality of women in the 20s, 30s, and 40s, and in countries with very high infant mortality, fertility declines might lower such mortality as well.

To illustrate, consider a population with low mortality, with, for example, an expectation of life at birth of 70 years. If high fertility levels prevail for half a century, such a population would show a median age of about 24 years, over 40% would be under age 15, and less than 5% over 65. With the low fertility levels now typical of industrialized countries, the median age would approach 40, only 20% would be under 15, and more than 15% over age 65. In contrast, changes of comparable magnitude in mortality would have only minor effects on age structure (Coale, 1957).

The Momentum of Population Growth

One of the characteristics of population growth that is now firmly established in demography is that of *demographic momentum*. Simply stated, this is the tendency of populations that have been growing to continue to do so for many decades after they have experienced fertility declines to low levels.

Demographic momentum arises out of the feedback between fertility, age structure, and crude birth and death rates. As noted above, a high-fertility population produces a relatively youthful population, that is, a population that is 40–50% children. If fertility then declines to low levels in such a population, there is a lengthy time lag before the number and crude rate of births similarly decline, because there is such a large concentration of young girls who will be reaching the age of reproduction over the several decades following the fertility decline. Put another way, demographic momentum arises from the fact that declines in the crude rate of natural increase lag behind declines in the intrinsic rate.

These distinctions are of fundamental significance to an appreciation of the fear of population decline. For often the feared decline is intrinsic rather than actual and can be perceived only through the analytic tools of demography or through the empirical simulations represented by population projections.

Population Projections

Population projections represent simply the playing out into the future of certain assumptions about the course of fertility, mortality, and migration. They emphatically are not predictions or forecasts, though they may be (and often are, sometimes inappropriately) employed as such. Assuming arithmetical accuracy, the utility of a projection is determined solely by the soundness of its central assumptions. If the assumptions represent plausible futures, then the projections do as well; if they do not, the projection is of little use and possibly seriously misleading.

Consider, for example, the case of a typical industrialized country, in which the intrinsic rate of natural increase is slightly negative and the crude rate slightly positive. Which natural increase would be most appropriate to assume for the coming 50 years? Should one assume another baby boom, as some scholars predict, or will below-replacement fertility persist, as others believe? In fact, no one can know the answers to these questions, yet any demographic projection must make assumptions in the absence of such knowledge.

The population projections prepared at the height of concern about population decline in the 1930s are now known to have been seriously deficient as predictions. Yet, to be fair to their authors, there was no way that anyone in the 1930s could have known that a recovery in fertility would occur in the 1950s. While it may be true that available techniques for studying future fertility intentions have improved since the 1930s, it is also true that the capacity to regulate fertility is now far more widespread than it was five decades ago. This implies an ironic conclusion: Our capacity to predict rationally the future course of fertility may have decreased, as the capacity of individual couples to effect rational control over their fertility has increased.

The misadventures of the demographic forecasters of the 1930s, coupled with the realization of our incapacity to predict future fertility behavior, has meant that few if any demographers are prepared to interpret long-term population projections as forecasts. Instead, the utility of projections is to illustrate the future effects of alternative assumptions about future demographic trends.

Period versus Cohort Rates

The distinction between the period and cohort concepts of demographic rates is important and needs to be clarified. The period rate is the conventional form, in which rates are calculated for a given time period, typically a calendar year. The cohort concept calculates demographic rates on the basis of behavior of generations or age groups over their lifetimes.

I. THE NATURE OF POPULATION DECLINE

Demographic measures such as the net reproduction rate can be formulated in either way. Period rates for current populations are usually "synthetic" in that they combine the behavior of a set of different age groups into the behavior of a hypothetical cohort; this is a weakness, in that it represents the behavior of no single cohort. However, such period rates have the advantage over true cohort measures in that they can be calculated for a given time period, while the cohort rate applies only to an age group of people over many years, and cannot be calculated completely until they have completed the bulk of that lifetime.

Like crude and intrinsic rates, both period and cohort rates are important and useful for different purposes, while at the same time there are dangers in mistaking one for the other. Indeed, this is one of the factors that underlay the striking but misbegotten predictions of the 1930s. Relatively new measures such as period net reproduction rates were misunderstood to be accurate reflections of underlying cohort rates. It was not understood then that period fertility rates can be heavily distorted by changes in the timing of reproduction while the underlying cohort rates might change little or not at all. Consider, for example, an extreme case in which all births for 1986 are deferred into 1987. The period net reproduction rate in 1986 would be 0, while that for 1987 would be much higher than otherwise. Yet by the end of their reproductive lifetimes, the cohorts of reproductive age in these 2 years might register identical figures for completed fertility.

It should be apparent, therefore, that the term *population decline* may refer to not one but many phenomena. To help avoid further mystification, let us list the following meanings of population decline, examples of all of which will be found in subsequent chapters:

1. a decline in the aggregate size of a population;
2. a decline in the crude rate of population growth;
3. a decline in natural increase or in the crude rate of natural increase;
4. a decline in the crude birth rate;
5. a decline in total or age-specific fertility rates;

6. a decline in the net reproduction rate or the intrinsic rate of natural increase;
7. a decline in the net reproduction rate or intrinsic rate of natural increase to levels below replacement;
8. a decline in desired or expected family size among young couples;
9. a decline in the proportion of young people and an increase in the proportion of old people in a population, or an aging of the population;
10. a decline in subjectively defined attributes of a society with a growing population, for example, innovation, mobility, risk-taking, and optimism; and an increase in subjectively defined attributes of an aging population, for example, conservatism, immobility, risk-aversion, and pessimism.

Few writers on population decline have bothered to identify to which of these levels their thoughts have been directed. Hence a rigorous and dispassionate approach to population decline requires the unravelling of knots of conjecture and confusion tied over the past century. It is to this theme that we turn in the next two chapters.

Demography and International Politics, 1870-1945

INTRODUCTION

Clarity about population questions today requires an understanding both of what has occurred in demographic terms over the past century and of how these occurrences have been perceived by contemporaries in a variety of settings. Let us consider first a brief overview of the course of vital events over the recent past before turning to our primary question of how such trends have been interpreted.

THE EUROPEAN DEMOGRAPHIC TRANSITION

The period stretching from the middle of the eighteenth century to the present includes what contemporaries and later observers recognized as perhaps the most profound set of economic and demographic transformations in history. Most of these are well known: the industrial revolution, leading to extraordinary economic advance; the rise and fall of European imperial power; the two great world wars; the revolutions in medical care, transportation, and communication; and the so-called post–industrial revolution of the past decade during which the technology and service sectors of the Western economy expanded rapidly.

No less profound was the major transformation of demographic behavior and characteristics that occurred over the same period. This is known to demographers as the ''demographic transition'' or the "vital revolution." In a span of not more than two centuries, and especially since about 1870, the countries of what is now called the North (i.e., Europe, North America, Japan, Australia, and New Zealand) registered substantial reductions in both mortality and fertility. For example, infant mortality in England and Wales declined from 154 deaths per 1000 live births in 1861 to 21 in 1961. Over the same years, the expectation of life at birth for males rose from 40 to 68 years (Preston, Keyfitz, and Schoen, 1972). With varying timing patterns, mortality declines of similar magnitude occurred in most other countries of the North.

Fertility also declined dramatically and universally in these countries. The harbingers of fertility decline were France and the United States, but between 1870 and 1940 virtually every country in the North had experienced a fertility decline on the order of 50%.

So substantial and universal were these declines in mortality and fertility that they gave rise to a descriptive interpretation sometimes presented as an explanatory model, known as the *theory of the demographic transition*. In fact, it is doubtful whether this theory was ever truly a theory at all (i.e., a set of hypotheses with predictive force), but this did not prevent its widespread dissemination as a key to an understanding of trends in vital rates.

According to demographic transition theory, rates of human mortality and fertility are functions of the fundamental economic and social changes of modernization or development. This theory describes three broad historical stages of human mortality–fertility experience. Stage I is said to characterize all (or nearly all) non-industrial societies: It is marked by an equilibrium of high mortality and high fertility over the long term. Mortality is erratic depending upon weather, epidemics, and the like, but over the long term mortality is high—an unavoidable situation in the absence of modern sanitation, health care, and agricultural production. By definition, any population surviving Stage I mortality levels must have established a regime of comparably high fertility, with such fertility levels sustained normatively and socially. Hence, in such a traditional society, high fertility is deeply institutionalized and slow to change. Nonetheless there is a fundamental asymmetry in this equilibrium, in that the high mortality levels are seen as uncontrollable evils, while the institutionalized regime of high fertility is seen as a positive good, with strong support provided through the traditional family and kin structure. Hence, as knowledge of means to reduce mortality is acquired, it is more readily accepted than is knowledge concerning means of fertility control.

This asymmetry leads to Stage II of the demographic transition, characterized by declining mortality while fertility remains at the high socially sanctioned levels. As a result, there is a period of sustained population growth resulting from the unprecedented surplus of births over deaths.

Finally, in Stage III of the transition, the equilibrium of slow or no growth is reestablished, as fertility control is adopted and fertility rates decline downward toward the levels of mortality. The proponents of transition theory posited a lag of several decades between the onset of Stage II and the appearance of Stage III, given the slow-to-change nature of social and cultural institutions. In developed nations, ultimately these institutions are modified by the fundamental transformations accompanying the industrial and urban revolutions of the nineteenth century. The family's role is purportedly weakened in almost every respect, according to this school of thought: in production, in consumption, in education, and in recreation. Since family structure is by far the most important institution supporting high fertility, this reduction in the centrality of the family supposedly weakens support for high fertility. At the same time, the growth of widespread or compulsory education reduces the economic value of the children because it removes children from the work force. People also gradually realize that infant and child mortality have declined and that fewer births are therefore required to achieve a given number of live offspring.

So much for the "theory." It would be charitable to say that there is considerable doubt and debate as to the adequacy of demographic transition theory as an explanation of the dramatic changes in demographic behavior over the past two centuries. Some propositions of transition theory have been supported by empirical test, for example, the generalization that mortality declines usually precede fertility declines (they do, though not in every case studied). However, it has also been discovered with some surprise that European fertility levels were far from uniformly high prior to the onset of sustained fertility decline. Part of this variation is attributable to differences in marriage patterns, but even when we make allowances for nuptiality, there is still no reason to retain the notion of a uniform high-pressure equilibrium in traditional societies. In addition, the social and economic factors (industrialization, urbanization, education, etc.) confidently put forward as explanatory variables of population change do not "explain" anything with precision. While some of these socioeconomic factors were associated with (though did not necessarily cause) fertility decline in some countries, in other countries such relationships are not at all apparent. Moreover, in many settings there appear to have been regional clusters of fertility behavior corresponding more to cultural and linguistic than to socioeconomic characteristics. Hence empirical testing of the theory of the demographic transition has led to considerably greater caution about its explanatory power than had prevailed before such tests were undertaken (see Coale, Anderson, and Harm, 1979; Knodel, 1968, 1974; Lesthaeghe, 1977; Livi Bacci, 1971, 1977; Teitelbaum, 1984).

The sustainable components of transition theory have been outlined by Coale (1973, p. 53) in the form of three broad *preconditions* for a substantial decline in fertility within marriage:

> 1) Fertility must be within the calculus of conscious choice. Potential parents must consider it an acceptable mode of thought and form of behavior to balance advantages and disadvantages before deciding to have another child—unlike, for example, most present day Hutterites or Amish, who would consider such calculations immoral, and consequently do not control marital fertility.
> 2) Reduced fertility must be [seen as] advantageous. Perceived social and economic circumstances must make reduced fertility seem an advantage to individual couples.
> 3) Effective techniques of fertility reduction must be available. Procedures that will in fact prevent births must be known, and there must be sufficient communication among spouses and sufficient sustained will, in both, to employ them successfully.

Of course, such preconditions are necessary rather than sufficient bases for fertility decline. We still cannot use the theory of the demographic transition as a model of past demographic change or as a predictor of future trends in the developing world. Hence, on the basis of many decades of scientific scrutiny, it is possible to account for the sustained fertility decline of the industrialized world in only the most general way. No set of propositions is capable of encompassing the diversity and complexity of the past century-plus of demographic change. The most fundamental of demographic transformations remains in many respects unexplained, and its relevance as a guide for future demographic change, ambiguous. It is not surprising, therefore, that reactions to demographic developments have been so diverse over the past century, since many of the causes of fertility trends remain a mystery to this day.

STRATEGIC DEMOGRAPHY, 1870–1914

In 1935, Gaston Bouthoul, professor at the École des Hautes Études Sociales in Paris and a specialist on population questions, succinctly summarized the character of much writing on the subject, including his own. Discussions of population dynamics, wrote Bouthoul, are frequently marred by the injection into them of "preconceived ideas, and of preconceived political ideas above all. One could say that in France the vast majority of works bearing on population are forms of special pleading, speeches for the defence, more or less masked" (1935, p. 7).

The content of that defense, wherever in Europe it was formulated, depended in large part on the perception of threats to nation, class, or race, which often were expressed in demographic form. We can see the validity of Bouthoul's remarks by examining some writing on population in Western Europe, and by placing it in the dual context of military anxieties and international conflict on the one hand, and of fears of internal instability and class conflict on the other. We shall examine these themes separately in the next two chapters, although the overlap between them is considerable. Together they furnish evidence of how widespread were European apprehensions of political and demographic decadence and decline in the period between 1870 and 1945.

The mountain of literature produced on population questions in these years included as well a large body of Malthusian writing. But many advocates of restraint on population growth in other countries were at the same time worried about the implications of declining rates of population growth in their own. To some, depopulation was a form of unilateral disarmament and therefore inherently dangerous. The military significance of many Malthusian and anti-Malthusian arguments gave them an importance that many political leaders acknowledged.

A second group of writers, politicians, and scientists were more concerned about the internal implications of differential fertility between social classes. Here the analogy between internal and international instability was drawn frequently, especially by those who saw a common thread linking both aspects of social conflict. In the late nineteenth century, and still more after the Russian Revolution of 1917, these two sets of anxieties were mutually reinforcing and lay behind the upsurge of interest in the likelihood and consequences of depopulation.

As we shall see later in this chapter, fear of population decline also appeared in the interwar years in both Western and Eastern Europe. In Russia the military imperatives of Stalin's strategy of socialism in one country lay behind the pronatalist and antiabortion initiatives of the late 1930s, which brought the socialist and nonsocialist worlds together in an appreciation of the significance of population questions in an age of total war.

In sum, we should not be surprised that the subject of population decline still brings out the fears and hopes of contemporaries today. For, as the discussion in Chapters 2 and 3 show, it has done so for as long as people have been aware of its existence.

The French Connection

In France the military consequences of demographic change were discussed incessantly from the Franco-Prussian War until the Second World War. Even before 1870 the rise of Prussian power caused some thoughtful Frenchmen to ponder the political significance of their country's slow rate of population growth (Le Fort, 1869, pp. 462–481). After the crushing defeat of France in the war of 1870–1871, which created both Bismarck's German Empire and the French Third Republic, the population question became a permanent part of the rhetoric and, on occasion, the substance of French politics. The tone of much of this debate can be sensed from one of the earliest and most revealing statements linking war and population. Pierre Toulemont, a Jesuit priest, saw the debacle of Napoleon III's military campaign and the bloodshed surrounding the suppression of the Paris Commune as signs of divine chastisement of the French people for the sin of contraception (Toulemont, 1873, as cited in Roberts, 1973, p. 32n; see also Toulemont, 1872). The upsurge of pietism after the events of 1870–1872, which has left as its monument the Basilica of Sacré-Coeur in Montmartre (Gadille, 1967, vol. II, pp. 229ff), gave such statements a popular force at a time when Catholics and other French conservatives were unable to face more concrete explanations of the failure of their class and country.

German writers reinforced the urgency of attempts to explain—or rather to explain away—the sources of French weakness in European affairs, so blatantly demonstrated on the battlefield of Sedan. Typical of the brash chauvinism and hauteur of the spokesmen of the new Reich was the boast of the distinguished ancient historian, Theodor Mommsen, whose work on Rome gave him what was taken as special insight into the character of declining, once-glorious powers. At Rome in 1878, Mommsen is supposed to have said, "Another German invasion, and all that will remain of France is a bad memory" (Bouthoul, 1935, pp. 9–10).

The sentiment behind these inflated, and yet to the French sadly plausible, remarks was taken to heart by one of the most prolific writers on the military consequences of population decline, Paul Leroy-Beaulieu, professor at the Collège de France and editor of *L'Économiste français*. In 1881 he wrote in his journal that France had to turn to colonial politics; continental politics were beyond the strength of her enfeebled people. "It takes courage," he wrote,

> to tell the truth to one's country and to destroy those illusions that will bring us new reverses and new catastrophes. In the presence of a Germany of 45 million inhabitants who will be 60 million in 20 years and 80 million in 50 years, and who can count on the loyalty of the Austrian populations, all the hopes of armed revenge are chimeras, sentimental and patriotic delusions, singularly dangerous for our country. (p. 566)

The annexation of Tunisia, he argued, was a step in the direction of national glory, more appropriate to France than a suicidal attempt to regain by arms Alsace and Lorraine (Leroy-Beaulieu, 1881). In his review of the 1881 census, the French Minister of the Interior, M. Goblet, voiced similar fears of French weakness. As *The Times* (London) put it, "There are not wanting now Frenchmen who look on the decreasing population as but one among many signs of national degeneracy, and are ready to exclaim hopelessly, 'Finis Galliae' " (16 January 1883, p. 3).

In all these counsels of gloom, we can observe as well the tendency to presume, rather than to prove, the causal link between demographic and military or political change. In the period before the full mechanization of warfare, it was understandable that many people assumed that military strength meant numerical superiority. What is less defensible was the reduction of major and complex questions of international politics to the level of mere reflections of vital statistics. Even Arsène Dumont, an anticlerical Republican demographer who shared few of Leroy-Beaulieu's conservative opinions, argued in 1890 that "a nation must have a population dense enough to keep stable an equilibrium with her neighbours." This France was unable to do, and as a result the standard-bearer of Republicanism and free thought was "at the mercy of monarchical and reactionary Europe" so long as France suffered from the "disease" of low natality (Dumont, 1890, pp. 57, 64).

British observers drew similar conclusions. One writer commented in 1902 that "France's old desire for revenge upon Germany has now probably lost much of its strength" because of her demographic weakness (Schooling, 1902, pp. 232, 237). Perhaps he would have been closer to the mark if he had said that the national spirit was willing, but the national flesh was too weak. This was the essence of numerous remarks in the decade prior to the First World War. One alarmed Frenchman put the following words into the mouth of an unnamed German professor, who surveyed the provisional results of French population movements in 1907 and concluded, "More coffins than cradles: this is the beginning of the end" and again, "Finis Galliae. Thus disappear by their own fault people who tamper with the fundamental laws of life" (Savant, 1909, p. 242). A similarly lugubrious message was stated by another observer obsessed by the link between military and demographic affairs, Alfred de Foville, president of the Académie des Sciences Morales et Politiques. "Militarily speaking," he wrote in 1909,

we have an increase in feebleness which accounts for the growing scantiness of our annual conscription, while abundant reinforcements grow in the armies in contrast to which, we have been unable to keep pace since 1870. That being so, what can our sons and grandsons hope for in future conflicts, regardless of how valiant they may be? (pp. 7–8)

Many other writers shared this sense of impending armed conflict as international tension increased in the decades prior to the First World War. Such apprehensions brought the links between military matters and demography into sharp relief in several countries. Adding to this atmosphere of gloom was disturbing evidence of military corruption and incompetence. The Dreyfus affair in France and the performance of the British army against what amounted to a handful of South African settlers in the Boer War exposed serious deficiencies in the military organization of both countries. In the aftermath of both episodes we can find additional evidence of the tendency for contemporaries to find in demography a recipe for the revival of military power or indeed of national survival itself.

What emerges most clearly from these debates is that the particular character of such exercises in what may be termed *strategic demography* depended in large part on the organization of military service. In France, conscription helped concentrate attention on questions of quantity and the need to increase the birth rate to cope with the German threat. In pre-1914 Britain, a voluntary system of military enlistment gave precedence to questions of quality and the need to improve the fitness of the nation as a whole, and in particular the fitness of those strata within the working class from which recruits came. Of course, in both countries there were those who mixed the two approaches, but by and large there was a fundamental contrast between the French obsession with fertility and the British emphasis on public health and mortality in the popular debate on population and military matters in the years prior to the First World War.

Let us consider the military equation that underpinned all such discussions in France. The basic problem, of course, remained that of German manpower. In 1906, for example, approximately 1.2 million men were called up in Germany, over 500,000 at age 20 and 670,000 men who had been deferred in previous years. In contrast, the French could muster in the same year only 368,000 recruits, of whom 318,000 were 20-year-olds and 40,000 were previously deferred men. The Germans, having more than three times the number of men from whom to choose front-line soldiers, actually could afford to send home more than 55% of the men called up on the grounds that they were needed as wage earners by their families. Another 16% went into the reserves. About half went to the *Ersatzreserv* (supplementary reserve) for (1) fit men not needed, (2) temporarily unfit men, or (3) men fit only for garrison duty. The remainder went to the *Landsturm* (civil guard). Such men did have something seriously wrong with them, such as blindness in one eye, heart disease, partial deafness, or deformities. But on the principle that anyone who could follow an active life as a civilian potentially could also do so in uniform, these recruits were not rejected outright but placed on a list to be called up only if the nation were in danger. That left only 3% of all those conscripted who were rejected on medical or moral (i.e., criminal) grounds. After all this sifting of recruits, only 26% of the original cohort, or 278,000 men, joined the regular German army in that one year (Balck, 1910, pp. 567–573; Pollock, 1910, p. 465).

How different it was for France. In order to match the German army in the field, the French had to take two-thirds of the conscripted classes directly into the regular army. The luxury of returning hundreds of thousands of men to their civilian jobs and families was simply out of the question. Indeed, conscription raised the specter of a further decline in the birth rate, the deficiencies of which had caused the military manpower problem in the first place (Hunter, 1962, pp. 490–503). Furthermore, the Germans placed men with disabilities in their reserve units; the French had to take them in for active service, and budgeted for an 8% drop-out rate of men invalided soon after enlistment (Pollock, 1910, p. 465).

These problems were the reality out of which the French fear of population decline grew in the years prior to the First World War. While many observers may have exaggerated the peril, they certainly did not invent it. Table 2.1 shows clearly the numerical advantage of the pool of potential recruits in Germany before the First World War.

Illustrated postcards in France, an ingenious and popular form of propaganda, helped bring the message home. One showed a scene of five Germans bayonetting two Frenchmen; another featured large German babies looking down on their smaller French counterparts. Others called on Frenchmen and women to recall

Table 2.1

MALE POPULATION OF FRANCE AND GERMANY AROUND 1910[a]

Age group	France, 1911	Germany, 1910
0–4	1693	3923
5–9	1671	3714
10–14	1661	3471
15–19	1593	3149
20–24	1535	2807
25–29	1523	2509
30–34	1482	2406
35–39	1401	2096
40–44	1270	1813
45–49	1194	1537

[a]In thousands. Source: Mitchell (1980, pp. 46–47).

their patriotic duty, even on their honeymoon.[1] But even had such promptings been successful—which was not the case—and the birth rate had risen dramatically, no improvement in the French strategic situation could have been expected for a full 20 years. Pessimism and pronatalism were joined, it seemed, in an inextricable embrace.

In this same period the French army faced difficulties of another order, which further complicated the discussion of the strategic situation of the nation, difficulties that arose directly out of the Dreyfus affair. It may perhaps be useful to take a slight diversion from the analysis of French military manpower and the German threat, to examine a little-known (and in itself insignificant) by-product of the Dreyfus affair, in order to appreciate the full extent to which discussions of population questions in this period became entangled with the political and military quarrels of the day.

If any one man symbolized the struggle to expose the nefarious workings of an effete and corrupt military caste, more interested in defending each other than the nation through all the sordid byways of the Dreyfus affair, it was the novelist Émile Zola. Zola was the son of an Italian-born railway engineer and came to be the confidant of Cézanne and Manet. He was also the author of the 20-

[1]We are grateful to Marie-Monique Huss for drawing these splendid cards to our attention.

volume Rougon-Macquart cycle of novels, the earthy realism of which shocked the contemporary literary world. Through novels like *L'Assomoir* (The Gin Palace), *La bête humaine*, and *Germinale*, Zola came to be vilified by his conservative enemies as "that Venetian pornographer" and honored by his admirers as a pioneer of literary truthfulness.

Initially Zola took little interest in the arrest, trial, and conviction in 1894 of a minor officer of the General Staff, Colonel Alfred Dreyfus, on charges of selling military secrets to the Germans. But when after several years it became apparent that high officers were engaged in an elaborate cover-up of evidence exonerating Dreyfus and pointing to the real culprit, Major Esterhazy, a notorious Hungarian rake in perennial money trouble, Zola took a public stand. This landed him in trouble and secured him an honored place in the pantheon of the liberal conscience. Two days after Esterhazy was triumphantly acquitted of treason in a stage-managed trial on 11 January 1898, Zola published his celebrated '*J'Accuse*, an Open Letter to the President of the Republic' in the mass-circulation Parisian newspaper *L'Aurore*. It accused the French high command of having engineered Dreyfus's conviction and Esterhazy's acquittal and dared the army to bring him to trial for libel. This they promptly did and secured a conviction, but only at the expense of a thorough airing of the irregularities and contraditions in the proceedings against Dreyfus. On a legal technicality, Zola was reprieved, only to be faced by a second trial at Versailles in July 1898. Before the guilty verdict could be pronounced a second time, Zola's counsel devised an ingenious way to keep the issues raised in *J'Accuse* alive and to keep its author out of prison. By fleeing the country, the trial would still be incomplete, as it were, thus buying time and publicity for the cause. Zola successfully slipped out of Paris unnoticed and arrived in England on 19 July 1898. There he remained for the next 11 months (Burns, 1964, pp. 1–45, 48–62).

For our purposes it is what Zola did in exile that is of relevance. At a time of scandal involving the highest reaches of France's military community, at a time of violent controversy over how to balance the claims of national security against the principle of justice for the individual, at a time when France seemed to be divided, in the words of one English commentator, between "those sections of society who could read and write and those who found it preferable to watch and pray" (Guedella, 1943, p. 269, as cited in Porch, 1981, p. 60), Zola sat down in his suburban London retreat to write an extraordinary novel about fertility, entitled *Fécondité*. Using material brought over secretly by his mistress and their two children (his official marriage remained childless), Zola constructed a labyrinthine tale of virtue and vice, which served as a paean to population growth, a patriot's vision of an abundant future for France secured through the triumph of fruitfulness and maternity over selfishness and sterility. This novel was the first of a projected series of four uplifting novels, or *évangiles* (gospels), announcing Zola's social religion of the future, in which reconciliation through fertility, work, truth, and justice would be proclaimed. His death in 1902 left this task unfinished and gives to these works something of the character of a last testament (Hemmings, 1977, chs. 18–20).

Fécondité is the history of a family. Mathieu Froment, a Parisian metal worker, marries at age 20 a young girl of 17, Marianne, whose parents had been killed by Arabs in Algeria and who was the poor cousin of the owner of a factory of agricultural equipment in which Froment worked. Together they struggle in adverse conditions to raise a rapidly growing family.

All the more-prosperous people who surround them deride their fruitfulness and devote themselves to egotistical and vicious pursuits. Beauchêne, the factory owner, is a vulgar Malthusian and a hypocrite, who blames the poor for their poverty. Beauchêne fathers only one legitimate (and sickly) child to keep in his family all he has accumulated. On the side, though, he seduces one of the young girls in his factory, Norine Moineaud, the daughter of an aged fitter. When her pregnancy becomes an embarrassment, out she goes.

Seraphine, the sister of Beauchêne, is a wicked and unmarried woman, dedicated to pleasure, who tries to lure Mathieu into her net, but without success. Slightly lower down the social order, the chief accountant of the factory, Morange, and his social-climbing wife, behave like good petits bourgeois and fear fertility as an obstacle to advancement. Madame Morange later dies tragically at the hands of an abortionist.

When Mathieu and Marianne decide to escape from this den of urban iniquity to work and later to purchase a farm named Chantebled, they continue to encounter decadence and sterility. Lepailleur, the miller, hates rural life, and after his only son dies of a dissolute life in Paris, his wife commits suicide. The Angelins, a frivolous couple dedicated to their private joys, postpone parenthood indefinitely; we shall meet them again. Local notables advocate contraception and pour scorn on the Froments and their brood. None of this has the slightest effect on the happy couple who continue to procreate at a steady pace. At one point in the middle of the novel, Marianne delivers at the rate of one child every two pages. Fifteen healthy children thrive in an environment of love and work.

In the meantime, back in Paris, the hereditary wages of sin are about to be paid. Beauchêne's cherished son dies of galloping consumption, but Zola notes, ''In reality his death was simply the final decomposition of impoverished, tainted bourgeois blood.'' The grief-stricken and slightly deranged mother finally decided to unmask her husband's debauchery and thereby to bring him down. She searches for the child borne by Norine Moineaud. In this quest she enlists the help of Mathieu, who knew about the scandal from the start, made sure that Beauchêne paid for a hospital delivery, and had then kept a discreet silence about it all. Together they scour the nests of wet nurses to find the one who had taken charge of Norine's son. They find a host of haridans, whose callousness and brutality to the children they receive is responsible for the deaths of many of them. But Beauchêne's child Alexandre had survived, only to disappear into the Parisian demiworld of street gangs and petty thieves. When he learns that inquiries are being made about him, he returns to his mother as an adolescent thug and prepares the stage for the fatal mugging of none other than Madame Angelin, childless, reduced to poverty, but dedicated to helping Norine Moineaud to survive.

The corruption of the family is completed as the murderer's mother turns murderess. Mathieu's son Blaise is a successful worker in the Beauchêne factory, which, Madame Beauchêne fears, he is bound to take over through sheer ability. This she prevents by leading him to the edge of a darkened shaft, down which he falls to his death. The accountant Morange witnesses the crime but is too spineless to speak out. The murder is in vain, though, as another Froment son steps forward to fill his brother's place.

To complete her husband's ruin, Madame Beauchêne brings Alexandre, her husband's bastard son, into the works. But all this is too much for Morange, who, contemplating suicide on a Parisian bridge, is rescued by one of Mathieu's granddaughters. Morange writes to Mathieu disclosing all, and then leads Alexandre to the same pit that claimed the body of Mathieu's son Blaise. Both Alexandre and Morange fall to their deaths. Madame Beauchêne, now completely mad, "poisoned by affection she was unable to bestow," dies, thus completing her family's tragedy.

Zola ends his novel by contrasting this gothic tale of self-inflicted grief suffered by the bourgeoisie with the celebration of the arcadian joys of the new peasant dynasty of Chantebled. Twenty years after the Beauchêne disaster, an army of 158 children, grandchildren, and great-grandchildren, as well as unnumbered great-great-grandchildren descend on the farm to mark the seventieth wedding anniversary of Marianne and Mathieu Froment. In the midst of the festivities, a grandson they had never seen appears. He is Dominique, whose father Nicholas had settled years before in Africa, "the other France", "the future France" to the development of which he calls the last of the Froment sons. With their help and that of similarly fertile sons and daughters of the soil, Dominique proclaims, "We shall swarm and swarm and fill the world." And thus, Zola affirms, the victory of patriotic procreation will be complete, and the Froments of this world will at last be able to take the rest they so conspicuously deserve.

Why did Zola write this novel, and why in particular did he choose this occasion to do so? His interest in population questions is muted but evident in many of his early novels. But by the late 1890s he felt sufficiently concerned to become a founding member of the National Alliance for the Growth of the French Population. After several forays into journalism on the subject of depopulation, he decided that a novel was the only way to reach the masses and set about researching the subject of infant mortality (Baguley, 1978, ch. 2).[2] What seems to have happened is that the novel changed in the making since Zola made up his mind to tell a patriotic story

[2]Information about this phase of Zola's life can be found in Vizetelly (1899). Vizetelly's English translation of *Fécondité* appeared in that year; references in the text are to this translation.

at a time when the nation was virtually tearing itself apart over the Dreyfus affair. Hence infant mortality recedes into the background, and in its place abundant motherhood becomes the force to bind the nation together and to enable it to fulfill its national and international destiny.

There is nothing like *Fécondité* in English literature, and this is so because there has never been in Britain anything like the overwhelming consensus among French writers, academics, and politicians that a revival of fertility was crucial for the survival of the nation. We have noted the strength of pronatalist sentiment among conservatives and enemies of the Third Republic. But when we find men like Zola—Zola, the tribune of the republican conscience, the scourge of capitalist injustice, the chronicler of the sufferings of the downtrodden and the exploited—joining in the pronatalist chorus in a novel serialized first in the popular press at a time of national crisis, we can appreciate the extent to which demographic, political, and military concerns were intertwined in all shades of French opinion prior to the First World War.

There are many echoes of Zola's sentiments in the literature of the period. Precisely at the time Zola wrote *Fécondité*, René Bazin called for a return to the land in *La Terre qui Meurt*. The work of Paul Bourget contains, in an arch-conservative form, evidence of another literacy apotheosis of the family. In his novel *L'Étape*, which appeared in 1902, he proclaimed the need to return to the simple virtues of family, hierarchy, and the church in order to avoid the disorders that flowed from republican, egalitarian, and cosmopolitan ideas.[3] A much more complex position was advanced by the equally widely read but considerably more liberal author (and colleague of Bourget in the French Academy), Eugène Brieux. In plays like *Maternité* and *Les Trois Filles de Monsieur Dupont*, Brieux excoriated the hypocrisy of the bourgeoisie. In public they carried the pronatalist flag; in private, they cared little for the heavy burdens faced by large working-class families, or even worse, they shunned unmarried mothers like the plague while forcing their own wives not to procreate.

The purpose of writers like Brieux and Zola was in part to popularize ideas of reform that would help save infant lives as well as

[3]Bowman (1925) is a good introduction to the early novels of Paul Bourget.

to encourage Frenchmen to have large families. We must set this literature of social criticism, therefore, in a long tradition of public concern over the problem of infant mortality. As early as 1862, the Ministry of the Interior had set up an investigation into infant mortality rates. Five years later the French Academy of Medicine appointed a commission on infancy, which became a permanent body in 1870. Four years later the celebrated *Loi Roussel* was passed, which required the registration and inspection of children sent out to wet nurses. The provision of cheap and clean cows' milk for infants whose mothers were unable to breastfeed them was pioneered in Paris in 1893. In 1892 the first prenatal clinic was established at the Charté Hospital, and the first milk dispensary was opened a year later by Dr. Variot at Belleville. Such measures were aimed at reducing foundling and other infant mortality rates of horrific magnitude. For example, in 1857 a British observer reported that "in Lyons and Parthenay, when children were suckled at the breast, the mortality was respectively 33.7% and 36% whereas in Paris, Rheims, and Aix, where they were brought up by hand, it was respectively 50.3%, 63.9%, and 80%" (Hewitt, 1958, p. 139). Earlier, the *Lancet* reported on a French hospital using artificial feeding methods in which 78% of infants died before the age of 1 (Phelps, 1913, pp. 132–183).

With this backdrop, we can see why French experiments in promoting infant health and welfare were well in advance of similar developments in Britain and other European countries. (See the admiring remarks of McCleary, 1905.) Equally, there was nothing on the statute books of the major powers to compare to the French Public Health Law of 1902, which required local authorities to investigate conditions in areas of high infant mortality. (Shapiro, 1981, pp. 14–15; see also Monod, 1904, for full details.)

The fear of population decline certainly helped popularize these campaigns to improve public health. Indeed, in all public discussions of population problems, the intrinsic value and national importance of the saving of child life were never doubted. The founders of the National Alliance for the Growth of the French Population chose that name precisely to make room in their organization for those concerned with the preservation of infant health and the struggle against infant mortality (Talmy, 1962, p. 68n). In 1902 the French senate appointed an extraparliamentary commission to study the problem of depopulation, and in its deliberations full attention was given to questions of mortality (Talmy, 1962, p. 102).[4] In the aftermath of the 1911 census, which showed an excess of deaths over births, and with the German problem highlighted by growing international tension, a second commission on depopulation was appointed, and again mortality problems were fully discussed. But in all these deliberations, and in many other writings, we still see a pronounced tendency to deplore high rates of infant mortality but to declare that the decline in fertility was the real evil sapping the vitality of the nation (Talmy, 1962, pp. 127–131).[5] In the words of Auguste Isaac, an activist in the family movement and later Minister of Commerce after the First World War, ''I do not believe that laws or hygienic measures can change anything. What governs population is natality; what determines natality are above all moral questions (Talmy, 1962, p. 131).

While few took quite such an extreme position on the matter, it is still true that movements in vital statistics in this period provided some justification for this viewpoint. In 1900, crude death rates in Germany and in France were almost identical, at about 22 per 1000. But whereas in Germany the crude birth rate stood at the level of 36 per 1000, that of France was down to a mere 21 per 1000. Here is the origin of the contrast in population growth rates and in that popular emphasis on fertility which we have found in the melodramatic fiction of Zola, as well as in the writings of many other authors, academics, scientists, and politicians, and which gave French opinion on population questions its characteristic flavor in this period.

The British Connection

When we cross the English Channel, a strikingly different mixture of elements appears in the pre-1914 debate on population. While pronatalist sentiment was widespread in Britain, the em-

---

[4]See also Beale (1911) for a list of members of the extraparliamentary commission and for summaries of its reports, which were never officially published. The journal *Revue Hebdomadaire* published a series of articles in 1909 that contained some of the commission's findings.

[5]For a much-cited earlier statement of the same position, see Richet (1982, p. 605).

phasis in popular debate was more on the "quality" of the race than upon aggregate growth rates per se. This distinction was made abundantly clear in the aftermath of the Boer War, when many concerned individuals responded to the military shortcomings of the campaign by calling for a searching inquiry into the health of the population, and especially of the working-class men from whom the army was recruited.

The revelation of shockingly high rejection rates of at least 40% of recruits in this period made possible the passage of a series of reform proposals for the protection of infant and child life. In rapid succession, the Liberal government of 1906 enacted measures for the medical inspection and feeding of schoolchildren and for the notification of births to local medical officers of health, who would be able to direct health visitors to people needing immediate medical or paramedical attention. The first state maternity benefit was instituted a few years later as part of the 1911 National Insurance Act (Gilbert, 1966, ch. 3; Searle, 1971, ch. 2).

Just as in the French case, though, such action could reap military benefits only in the long term. For the immediate future, the most pressing problem highlighted by the furor over recruitment was the stubborn survival of urban working-class poverty at a time when Britain was still the world's greatest economic power. What public hearings exposed were the miserable conditions in which thousands of poorly educated and unskilled slum dwellers lived, buffeted by the ebb and flow of the casual labor market. Armed forces recruited from this population were bound to be, in the eyes of these concerned observers, a fragile shield for the Empire.

The two forums in which these matters were debated were the hearings of the Royal Commission on Physical Training in Scotland, which sat between 29 April and 3 October 1902,[6] and the Interdepartmental Committee on Physical Deterioration, which sat between 3 December 1903 and 20 June 1904.[7] The briefs of these

[6]For the report of the Royal Commission on Physical Training in Scotland, see Parliamentary papers (hereafter P.P.), Cd 1507 (1903) xxx; for the evidence Cd 1508 (1903) xxx. All references to the evidence are cited hereafter as PTS.

[7]For the Report of the Interdepartmental Committee on Physical Deterioration, see P.P., Cd 2175 (1904) xxxii; for the evidence, Cd 2210 (1904) xxxii; for the appendices, Cd 2186 (1904) xxxii. All references to the evidence are cited hereafter as PDC.

committees were similar. They were to set out the facts of physical unfitness among the population as a whole, to try to determine whether or not things were getting worse over time, and to suggest ways to ameliorate or prevent physical deterioration.

Before briefly describing the main themes of these deliberations, it is perhaps useful to dwell for a moment on that highly charged phrase, "physical deterioration." No two commentators in Britain agreed on how to define or explain it. Most used the term *deterioration*, a physical term, roughly the opposite of *health*, but some made it carry a number of moral connotations as well, such as laziness, stupidity, and indifference to familial responsibilities. Some considered it a relative term, describing a descent from a preindustrial summit of sturdiness. Others used it as a term to describe the pathogenicity of the urban environment against which each new generation of slum dwellers had to struggle to survive. That infant mortality rates in the 1890s were on occasion higher than those recorded in the 1850s was to some a prime indicator of deterioration. Finally, many commentators used the term in an international context, to compare the aggregate physical strength or belligerent potential of competing imperial powers.

None of these definitions was clear or precise, and inevitably so, since what they really described was a sense of unease among some articulate middle-class professionals about the future of a nation dominated numerically (if not politically) by the urban working class. It was this feeling that the rejection rate among recruits brought to the surface and that lay like a cloud over the deliberations of learned inquiries and meetings after the turn of the century.

The key problem that preoccupied these public hearings was that unskilled laborers constituted the great majority of military recruits. Most witnesses attributed the physical and mental "deficiencies" and the high infant and child mortality rates among unskilled laborers to early childhood deprivation. While the location of degeneracy primarily in one social strata enabled both committees to reject fears of *national* deterioration, high fertility rates among the worst-off sections of the population seemed to these learned gentlemen to bode ill for the nation's future. Here was a crucial element in the British discussion of the connections linking fertility, mortality, and military power, expressed frequently in doubts as to the vitality of the imperial race.

The assertion that the British army provided a home only for the outcasts of British society was never seriously challenged in these inquiries. But one fundamental problem appeared that undercut attempts to use military recruitment statistics as a guide to the physical state of even one stratum within the working class, let alone that of the nation as a whole. Recruiting officers testified that the trade cycle changed the social composition of enlistment in such a way as to alter the mean physical character of the cohort presenting itself for military service. When times were good, only the dregs of society came forward. Their physical profile was, as many noted, appalling. But ironically, when times were bad, the army got better men who were unable to find work or a steady income in any other way (PDC, qq 171, 435, 2188, 4040, 11003; PTS, q 8295). Recruitment statistics, therefore, could paint a perverse picture of prosperity yielding a deterioration in the physique of the unskilled, or of depression yielding an equally spurious improvement.

For this reason both committees shifted the angle of their inquiries away from military recruiting statistics to the causes of ill health among the infants and children of the urban poor from whom future recruits would be drawn. By doing so, they had to deal with the sociology of urban poverty, or in other words, with the fundamental distinction within working-class communities between the better-off "respectable" strata, who did not on the whole tend to join the army, and the worse-off "rough" strata, who did.

Dr. W. Leslie Mackenzie, a Scottish medical officer, provided a classic description of the contrast between the terribly malnourished children of the North Canongate School in Edinburgh and the physical condition of children in three other schools in the city (PTS, Report, appendix ix). What he and his colleague Professor Matthew Hay of Aberdeen showed the Royal Commission on Physical Training in Scotland was the existence within the urban population of an underclass, whose plight was not worse perhaps than that of their parents, but who were relatively even more deprived because they had not shared in the gains made over time by other sections of the working class. While the nation as a whole registered improvements in life expectancy as shown in the successive annual reports of registrars-general, this underclass had continued on the treadmill of malnutrition, overcrowding, and chronic disease.

2. DEMOGRAPHY AND INTERNATIONAL POLITICS, 1870-1945

Dr. Alfred Eichholz, a London school inspector, brought before the Interdepartmental Committee on Physical Deterioration a vivid example of the effects of malnutrition on children at school just across the Thames from Westminster, where the hearings were being held. A visit to the Johanna Street Board School in Lambeth uncovered the startling fact that, according to medical opinion, the physical condition of approximately 90% of the children there interfered with their ability to pursue their studies (PDC, qq 435ff). The state insisted on compulsory education for the nation's children; could it tolerate a situation where they were too sickly to benefit from it? The answer was clearly no, and the case for the medical inspection of children at school followed directly and forcefully from this one tangible example of the level of child health in Edwardian Britain.

What ought to be done about this substratum of the working population was a question that troubled many witnesses. No less an authority than Charles Booth, the author of *Life and Labour of the People of London,* pressed the case for emigration to labor colonies (PDC, q 987). Charles Loch of the Charity Organisation Society expressed his admiration for the way the German police helped control the urban poor and advocated a militia system for British boys (PDC, qq 10226, 10227). According to J. Struthers, assistant secretary to the Scottish Education Department, hooliganism was virtually nonexistent in Germany due to better policing and universal conscription (PTS, qq 154–155). And the thrust of most of the Scottish investigation of physical training was to develop the argument that military drill was a civilizing and rehabilitating force.

The idea that better wages would reduce the extent to which this underclass disturbed or disfigured the body politic was raised indirectly only by two witnesses to the Interdepartmental Committee on Physical Deterioration. The first was Seebohm Rowntree, author of *Poverty: A Study in Town Life,* in which he had popularized the distinction between primary and secondary poverty. He suggested that the committee seek the sources of national deterioration in the fact that between 3 and 4 million people in Britain could not afford to buy sufficient food to ensure a minimum of physical efficiency (PDC, qq 5039, 5265, 5350). Additional evidence along these lines was provided by H. J. Wilson, inspector of factories and workshops in Newcastle-upon-Tyne. The substandard heights and weights of children of workers in the jute mills of Dundee, he believed, were indicators of chronic malnutrition among the low-paid sector of the population (PDC, qq 1916, 1919, 1936).

Of course, the advocacy of better pay was not the concern of these committees, on which not a single working-class man or woman sat. Such a radical proposal would have served only to sink the hopes of rallying support for medical inspection or feeding programs in the schools, which were at least steps in the right direction.

No one pretended that such measures would solve the problem of the *residuum,* a term many contemporaries used as shorthand for the unskilled urban working class. Some hoped that the same decline in fertility that had reduced the birthrate among the more prosperous classes would eventually spread to the lowest orders as well. That such was not yet the case was the source of many complaints about the proliferation of the unfit, which we examine in Chapter 3. We can see the outline of these arguments in the words of Sir John Gorst, member of Parliament for Cambridge University and champion of state provision for the feeding of necessitous schoolchildren. He told the Interdepartmental Committee on Physical Deterioration that he was impressed with the idea "that the race is propagated in the greatest proportion by the least fit parts of it (PDC, q 11790). Sir Charles Cameron, medical officer of health for Dublin, lent the weight of his Irish experience to the view that the dregs were reproducing at a greater rate than the superior stocks (PDC, q 11017).

One year later, at a meeting of the British Association in Cambridge to advance the call by the Interdepartmental Committee on Physical Deterioration for an anthropometric survey of the race, Prime Minister Arthur Balfour added his voice to the chorus of alarm. He pointed out that the most enterprising members of the working class who rose through education and effort started immediately to limit their family size in a way their less successful neighbors avoided. He was led inevitably, he said, to the "rather melancholy conclusion that everything done towards opening up careers to the lower classes did something towards the degeneration of the race" (British Association, 1905, p. 26). We shall explore this theme further in Chapter 3.

STRATEGIC DEMOGRAPHY, 1914-1945

European Security

It must have come as a great surprise to these prophets of doom that a decade later, while the French held Verdun and the British withstood the carnage of the Somme and Passchendaele, virile Germany lost the war of attrition on the Western Front. But the fact that France's population growth rates still lagged behind Germany's at the end of the war and in the interwar years continued to trouble the French. As early as 1919, Prime Minister George Clemenceau injected a demographic note into the debate on ratification of the Treaty of Versailles:

> The treaty does not say that France must undertake to have children, but it is the first thing which ought to have been put in it. For if France turns her back on large families, one can put all the clauses one wants in a treaty, one can take all the guns of Germany, one can do whatever one likes, France will be lost because there will be no more Frenchmen. (*Journal Officiel: Débats du Sénat*, 11 Oct. 1919, pp. 1625-1626; as cited in Tomlinson, 1984)

Five years later, Prime Minister Poincaré drew the attention of the Congress of Republican Federations to the "military problems" that directly followed from demographic decline; international instability and *dénatalité* (a decline in birth rates) went hand in hand (*The Times* [London], 25 April 1924). A writer in *Germania*, the journal of the Catholic Center party in Germany, argued that such anxiety tied to demographic insecurity was the real reason for French *révanchisme* and general hostility over reparations and French occupation of the Rhineland (*The Times* [London], 26 Jan. 1924). Here again we see the tendency to find a demographic explanation for international developments that sidestepped what were, from the German point of view, more critical appraisals of European security problems.

A good example of what may be termed the "confusions of strategic demography" emerged in a discussion of the French occupation of the Rhineland in 1920, following the entry of German soldiers into the Ruhr. What shocked many observers on the left as well as on the right was the use of black Moroccan soldiers by the French to police a white population. The press was replete with fears of this unleashing of African sexuality on European womanhood (Reinders, 1968, pp. 1–28). But for our purposes, the most revealing comment was that of a progressive Labour member of the British Parliament, Sir Leo Chiozza Money. He reasoned that the fall in the fertility of native Frenchmen explained her use of black soldiers on the Rhine. "What a mournful problem it is," he lamented, "this of France believing herself forced to frame a great black army in anticipation of the failure of her white manhood" (Money, 1925, p. 89).

Whether or not this was true, it seems likely that the French strategic decision in the mid-1920s to retreat behind a Maginot line reflected the recognition that Germany could not be kept weak and that consequently defiance had to give way to defensiveness. By the mid-1930s advocates of rearmament believed that mechanization was the only hope for a country with insufficient manpower. This theme was developed in the defense debate in the Chamber of Deputies in late January 1937 by Paul Reynaud, an apostle of rearmament, soon to become minister of justice and later minister of commerce under Daladier. Reynaud reminded the chamber that "there is one factor that dominates all: the demographic factor" (*Journal Officiel: Débats du Chambre*, 28 Jan. 1937, p. 168).[8] In the dangerous international climate of that year, France appeared to him to be like a man of affairs who had contracted a dangerous illness and, in consequence, disregarded his health. Precisely because one French worker faced two German workers, rearmament had to be accelerated to enable the depleted French army to fight a mechanized war. This, in Reynaud's view, was the only war France could win.

Other deputies reiterated Reynaud's central theme, while on occasion diverging from his conclusions. Léon Archimhaud reminded his colleagues that "we can take from our marvellous colonial domain the troops needed to match Hitler and his 67 million Germans" (*Journal Officiel: Débats du Chambre*, 28 Jan. 1937, p. 214). Fernand Laurent, a deputy of the moderate right, indicted the government of the Popular Front for its inaction on demographic problems. While admitting that previous governments had

[8]We are grateful to Mrs. Pippa Temple for drawing this reference to our attention.

been equally negligent, he still held that immediate steps had to be taken to raise the birth rate. *"Dénatalité* isn't a health problem, it is a problem of national defense of the first order, perhaps the most important of all. Tomorrow it will be the problem of national defense in itself" (*Journal Officiel: Débats du Chambre,* 29 Jan. 1937, p. 246).

What these writers feared was that France was about to decline to the status of a second-rank power. Among her allies similar sentiments were voiced. Consider one thoughtful article written, perhaps with Foreign Office assistance, by the Paris correspondent of *The Times* (London) in early 1939. The writer saw in slow population growth rates the source of "the paralysis of French initiative" and "of the chronic depression from which she is suffering" (16 Jan. 1939). The reader might well wonder why Britain should fight alongside such a decadent partner. Thus a demographic case could be made out not only for rearmament but also, in this instance, for appeasement.

The fall of France in 1940 provided another opportunity to account for political and military failures on demographic grounds. The Vichy regime enthusiastically condemned the decadence of the Third Republic and enthusiastically embraced the pronatalism of the National Alliance for the Growth of the French Population. The editor of its bulletin proclaimed in August 1940 that "family questions now have an importance they never had in the past." This sidestepped the achievements of the Daladier government in passing in July 1939 a family code of unprecedented comprehensiveness. But what he probably had in mind was the inspiration of Pétain's slogan of collaborationism, "Work, Family, Country," which announced the victory of the collective over the individual conscience.

Like their Nazi protectors, Vichy politicians organized festivals of family culture. One was held at Rheims on Mothers' Day in 1941 under the patronage of Pétain himself. Medals for distinguished service were distributed: bronze for women with 5 children, silver for those with 7, and gold for those with at least 10 offspring (*Révue de l'alliance national contre la dépopulation,* July–Aug. 1941, pp. 249ff.). Throughout the period 1940–44, the preoccupation of Vichy with the purification of youth and the strengthening of what they believed to be the traditional values of the French family represented one of a number of lines of continuity between collaboration and pre-Second World War French politics.

Members of the Resistance publicly shared little with their collaborationist compatriots, except a conviction that a decline in natality lay at the heart of the fall of the grandeur of France. In a spirited call to Frenchmen to confront the population problem, which was "for France, the essential problem, the only real problem" (p. 9), Robert Debré and Alfred Sauvy wrote in 1946 that

> The terrible failure of 1940, more moral than material, must be linked in part to this dangerous sclerosis [resulting from low birth rates]. We saw all too often, during the occupation, old men leaning wearily towards the servile solution, at the time that the young were taking part in the national impulse towards independence and liberty. This crucial effect of our senility, is it not a grave warning? (p. 58)

For France, "depopulation carried with it, fatally, a general legacy of decadence" made infinitely worse by the fact that "the terrible ravages of the 1914–18 war among the best of our men were not repaired". This lowered the "quality of leadership" in the interwar years (Debré and Sauvy, 1946, p. 86).

In Chapter 3 we return to this theme of a "lost generation of elites" as one of the pillars of the widespread fear of "race suicide" over which many Europeans brooded in the first half of this century.

Imperial Power

Other Europeans cast their nets further afield to find the link between population and international politics in the imperial world. In Britain, as we have already noted, concern about the tenuous hold of a declining race over a far-flung empire was a recurrent theme. As Arthur Newsholme, a progressive and distinguished chief medical officer to the local government board put it: "It cannot be regarded as a matter of indifference whether the unfilled portions of the world shall be peopled by Eastern races (Chinese, Japanese, Hindoos etc.), by Negroes, by Sclavonic [sic] or other Eastern European peoples, by the Latin races, or by the races of Eastern Europe. . . . Every Briton will wish that his race may have a predominant share in shaping the future destinies of mankind" (Newsholme, 1906, pp. 57, 58).

2. DEMOGRAPHY AND INTERNATIONAL POLITICS, 1870-1945

Montague Crackanthorpe (1906), a conservative eugenicist, drew the parallel between the decline of natality in Rome and in Britain. With Gibbon, this author cried "Outraged Nature will have her revenges" (p. 1009).

Dampier Whetham, an even more conservative exponent of eugenics, voiced the standard pronatalist claim, with a eugenicist gloss, in his review of the rise in the marriage and birth rates in the first year of the 1914-1918 war in Britain. In his view both rates showed a sense of patriotism in the population among those who recognized that "the welfare of the country and the Empire depends on an adequate supply of satisfactory men and women" (1917, p. 230). In a similar vein, he had praised the strength of the German empire before the war, which was ultimately based on "the fact that her birth rate did not begin to fall systematically till twenty years later than that of Great Britain" (Whetham and Whetham, 1909, p. 131). And even then, in Germany, that decline had "not yet destroyed the old predominance of the stronger and more intellectual sections of the nation" (p. 132), the vanguard of an imperial race.

The same theme of imperial defense lay behind the establishment under the auspices of the National League of Life of an unofficial National Birth-rate Commission, which met intermittently between 1913 and 1926. The leading spirit behind its work was the Reverend James Marchant, a confirmed pronatalist, who summarized its mixture of military and imperial themes in a pamphlet that appeared in 1917. From the answer to this rhetorical question, "Would Germany have declared war on France if her population had been as large as Germany's?" he concluded, "In the difference between the number of coffins and the number of cradles lies the existence and persistence of our Empire (Marchant, 1917, pp. 10, 17).

Communism

In the same year as Marchant's pamphlet was published, the Russian Revolution added a new dimension and a new level of hysteria to the fear of population decline in Western Europe and elsewhere. In 1920, a prominent adventure novelist and pronatalist, Sir Rider Haggard, warned that unless Russian numbers were diminished, "directed by German skill and courage and aided by other sinister influences, what devastation might they not work upon the rest of Europe, should its manpower be depleted!" (Marchant, 1920a, p. 180). Chiozza Money saw revolution spreading in several directions at once. In China as elsewhere, he noted in 1925, "We have to reckon with the Bolshevist menace. The Soviet agents, emissaries as deadly as any dispatched of old by the sect of assassins, work eagerly to foment disorder, to make China a determining factor in world revolution" (Money, 1925, p. 78). And what was worse, "we have to consider the influence of Bolshevism in a world in which White Civilization is sufficiently in danger" without it (p. 97), because of declining fertility.[9]

The same fear troubled C. P. Blacker, a biologist and eugenicist, who pointed to the danger of the spread of Communism in the aftermath of the Russian Revolution, that "event which in 1917 cast her beyond the pale of Western Civilization" (1926, p. 72). Should another world war break out, the British Empire would have no hope of survival. Furthermore, "The seeds of revolution in Europe, by then more deeply sown, would germinate, and the present social order would come to an end" (pp. 77–78).

Less penetrating, but equally troubled, was a Swiss economist of Hungarian origin, who wrote in 1934 that "we must take note of the risk of another great invasion westward by the peoples of the East," whose inferior living conditions would "impel them westward" (Ferenczi, 1934, p. 368). He neglected to mention that, whatever other problems the Soviet Union faced in the 1930s, the terrible dislocation associated with the world economic crisis was not one of them. After the Second World War, a leading Catholic pronatalist, Halliday Sutherland, took up the by-now-familiar theme. In the Soviet Union, he noted in 1951, there was "an enormous population which might easily overflow into the underpopulated lands of less virile races. These towering facts make one wonder how any government in Western Europe could be so

[9]Money was also appalled by what he termed the "nationalization of abortion" in the Soviet Union.

senseless as to tolerate the preaching of contraception" (Sutherland, 1951, p. 33).

It probably would have shocked the anti-Communist brigades to learn that Stalin, too, was worried by a decline in the birth rate. On 4 May 1936, he spoke to the Academy of the Red Army on the subject of "Man, the Most Precious Capital" and urged all Russians to celebrate the joys of maternity and the pride of paternity, home, and marriage. A carefully orchestrated series of meetings and articles helped broadcast the new policy, which culminated in the passage of a law in June 1936 banning abortion. This was a supreme volte-face in Soviet policy. While official policy in the years after the revolution was to oppose contraception as a shabby Malthusian bourgeois tactic to help them hoard their wealth, he had had no objection to abortion, which was legalized as a woman's right by decrees in 1920 and 1925 and by law in 1924. Twelve years later, when Stalin had personally and massively contributed to Soviet depopulation and when a European war began to loom on the horizon, it was time for a change. Accompanying the banning of abortion was a substantial increase in support for maternal and child welfare.

After the German invasion of the Soviet Union in June 1941, the "Imperialists' war" suddenly became a "Peoples' war" requiring a further replenishing of the nation's human stocks. On 21 November 1941, the Presidium of the Supreme Soviet established a tax on celibates, childless citizens, or those with only one child. Three years later the presidium created the honorary title of "Heroic Mother" for women with large families, who were entitled to the decoration the "Glory of Motherhood" or the "Medal of Maternity" depending on how fertile they had been (Chambre, 1954, pp. 206–227; Schlesinger, 1960, pp. 251–274). The parallel with Vichy France is too clear to miss, and the enormous losses suffered by the Soviet Union in the war against Hitler provided a justification for pronatalism, which the minions of Laval and Pétain derived from the earlier carnage of the First World War.

The eugenics literature of Nazi Germany and Fascist Italy, which we shall briefly survey in Chapter 3, contained similar paeans to procreation. In addition, fascists had an enormous battery of "evidence" justifying on demographic and security grounds the oppression of "inferior" races at home and of "lesser" races abroad (Kuczynski, 1939).[10] But as we have seen, throughout the interwar years, they were certainly not alone in interjecting a powerful demographic component in the course of military discussions. Few European leaders in these years failed to succumb to the temptations of strategic demography.

[10]For the views of an Italian demographer sympathetic to fascism, see Gini, 1923, pp. 430-431. For German views, see Mosse, 1978.

Demography and Internal Politics, 1870-1945

THE EUGENIC APPROACH TO POPULATION DECLINE

When we turn to the subject of population decline as a theme in discussions of the internal politics of Western Europe and the United States in the period 1870–1945, we see two related but not identical fears expressed by a heterogeneous group of writers, scientists, and politicians. The first is anxiety over the eclipse of elites by the more prolific masses. The second is a worry over "pollution" of an indigenous population by immigration and/or miscegenation.

Most defenders of social inequality in Europe and America in this period shared a number of simple and widely held assumptions about racial characteristics and racial superiority, although not all those holding such racial views supported social inequalities. The reason is that the anti-elitism of some fascist movements distinguishes their outlook from that of some of their conservative allies. The Nazis, for example, argued that Aryan features and pure blood were the essence of the *Volk* (or nation) as a whole, and not the monopoly of only one class. For this and for other reasons, the place of traditional elites in the Nazi state was precarious, as many of them recognized sadly and belatedly. Fears of social submergence and racial decline frequently coincided, but were not fused.

This is not to deny the affinity between some sources of fascist thinking and the views of exponents of the fear of population decline, taken as the decline of elites. Consider a study of heredity and society written in 1912 by two English eugenicists, the Cambridge economist Dampier Whetham and his wife, Dorothy. They had just read Houston Stewart Chamberlain's book, *The Foundations of the Nineteenth Century,* which later became a minor classic of Nazi "thought." At a time of unprecedented industrial unrest in Britain, and during the controversy over the restriction of the veto power of the House of Lords, the Whethams (1912) found Chamberlain's message to be of profound importance. What had to be done in Britain as in Germany was to demonstrate that

> The great things of the world are accomplished by individuals who have a strong personality and by races which have a strong race-personality. Within the nation itself, the best work is done by groups or sections of the people that are easily recognized and have strongly marked characteristics. We have shown reason to believe that this differentiation of type into so-called classes, which is found in all successful national evolution, is essential to the maintenance of progress. (pp. 69–70)

But something had gone wrong in the development of class society in Britain: the superior "stocks" were not reproducing themselves. In consequence,

> Great men are scarce; the group personality is becoming indistinct and the personality of the race by which success was attained in the past, is therefore on the wane, while the forces of chaos are once more being manufactured in our midst, ready to break loose and destroy the civilization when the higher types are no longer sufficient in numbers and effectiveness to guide, control or subdue them. (p. 70)

Here we can savor the dark pessimism of elites under siege, and see encapsulated that mixture of fear of social unrest and a loss of mastery that marked the writings of many Europeans concerned with population decline.

A belief in demographic determinism suffuses the writings of many of those who addressed the problem of population decline in the period 1870–1945. The relatively lower fertility of elites compared to that of working people provided many with a useful account of the genesis of social instability, and even on occasion, of the downfall of "civilization." If contraception was a key subversive agent in contemporary history, then one could dispense with arguments about the destabilizing effects of poverty and inequality. Hence, for such writers, a simple form of demographic analysis could completely and conveniently displace social analysis.

Positive Eugenics

The original meaning of the term *eugenics* was the science of race improvement. In the late nineteenth century, the term *race* was used frequently as a synonym for nation; "the British race" and "the European race" are examples. It was also used in the way we take for granted today, that is, to describe a population of a distinct physical type or color of skin—"the Caucasian race" or "the Mongoloid race." Because of the highly charged character of the language of race today, it is perhaps best to be more precise than were the eugenicists in delineating their subject, and therefore we define it as the science of the improvement of the genetic stock of the human population or of subgroups within it. As such it constitutes a body of ideas and proposals of a positive kind, encouraging or stimulating the propagation of individuals and groups deemed to contribute to the well-being of the community, as well as a set of notions of a negative kind, restricting or eliminating the propagation of characteristics, individuals, or groups deemed detrimental.

Much has been written about the history of eugenics, largely because of the shadow cast on it by the experience of National Socialism in Germany (See Haller, 1963; Schneider, 1982, pp. 268–291; Searle, 1978). It is important to note, though, that many supporters of eugenics found both Nazism and what we understand today as racism to be completely repugnant, and that many politicians, scientists, and men of letters who were profoundly antifascist addressed themselves to the problem of race hygiene in the period under review. We are not dealing with the lunatic fringe when we survey the history of eugenics in Europe and America, and it is only by stripping away the categories of our present more egalitarian culture that we can appreciate the earlier meaning of eugenics and the extent to which it provided a language with which to express a fear of population decline.

The quest for ability or genius was a virtual obsession with many European writers in the late nineteenth century. Galton's influential book, entitled *Hereditary Genius*, which was first published in 1869, awakened an interest in the problem of the transmission of ability over time (see Cowan, 1972, pp. 380–412; Forrest, 1974; Galton, 1908). Many saw in this question the most important aspect of the decline of fertility. One case in point is the English Roman Catholic physician, J. W. Taylor. In 1906 he wrote of his belief that the "vicious and unnatural habits of the present generation" had led to a dearth of "men of surpassing genius" (p. 226). It is not surprising that Taylor was oblivious of the contemporary existence of Picasso, Freud, or Einstein, but the fact that they were alive at the time throws an ironic light on his conclusion that "our mischievous meddling with great natural forces" (p. 226n) has stripped the world of genius. Taylor believed that supreme ability, as in the cases of Shakespeare, Walter Scott, and John Wesley, occurred mainly in large families.

During the First World War, and in its aftermath, this theme of the demographic sources of the alleged dearth of ability in the modern world was translated into the cult of the "Lost Generation," the remembrance of social elites who fell in the Great War. There was some truth in the claim that the British upper classes suffered disproportionately heavy war losses, largely on account of the slaughter of the officer corps in the trenches. But since the vast majority of men who died in uniform were working-class, it is clear that the literary reverie for the young poets, philosophers, and politicians who fell in Flanders fields really arose out of fears of the decline of ability in European society. According to some, war losses helped complete the work that birth control had already begun, that is, to strip the European world of talent and thereby to place another nail in the coffin of European supremacy and that of its privileged classes (Winter, 1976, pp. 449–466).

Consider this comment made in 1917 by a correspondent in a British medical journal, the *Journal of Tropical Medicine and Hygiene*: that one-child privileged families who had lost their only sons in the First World War had been punished for their "loathsome practices," or in other words, for following "the foul teaching of family limitation" (1917, p. 238). Such remarks proliferated in a wide body of literature on the supposed "dysgenic character" of the war. As early as 1914, Dr. Caleb Saleeby provided a visual record of what he believed the war was doing to the race:

> Every afternoon when my work is done I go into Hyde Park, and I watch a small portion of Kitchener's Army [of volunteers] drilling, and I compare those splendid young men, everyone of whom I pay homage to in

my heart, with the washouts, dirty drunken, and diseased, whom no recruiting sergeant since time began wanted to look at a second time, lying about in the grass, and I realize the trash is remaining at home and the treasure is going away to be killed. (p. 5)

The very least England could do, he went on, was to protect the issue of the nation's "treasure" by supporting the soldiers' and sailors' wives who were pregnant and thereby were doing "equally good service for England" by giving birth to healthy babies (Saleeby, 1914, p. 5). Perhaps this modern variant of the old adage as to the proper role of women, "Lie back and think of England," can be traced, like so many other things, to the First World War.

Even those who pioneered family planning stressed the need to procreate ability, or in so many words, for the propertied classes to reproduce their own kind. Marie Stopes, the sponsor of the first birth control clinics in Britain, told the National Birth-rate Commission that she wanted to increase the fertility of the "better classes" because "in our class the children of the last twenty-five years are mentally and physically superior to those of the poorer and more thriftless of the working classes" (Marchant, 1920b, pp. 253, 255). The same opinion was voiced a few years later by Lucien March, president of the French Eugenics Society. He told an International Eugenics Conference in New York that "innate qualities" are greater in wealthier families than in poorer families (March, 1923, pp. 249–250). In 1930 a distinguished British biologist, R. A. Fisher (1930), added his weight to the argument that "a number of qualities of moral character" show "a relative concentration in the more prosperous strata of existing populations" (pp. 262–263). Leonard Darwin, fourth son of Charles Darwin, and president of the Eugenics Education Society, spent 30 years of his life propagating this idea (Darwin, 1926, p. 327; 1928, p. 67). C. P. Blacker, whose views we have cited above, made the similar claim in 1934 that those who "rise in the social scale exhibit socially valuable qualities which are largely innate and at least partly hereditary" (p. 74). Two years previously, a noted German racial biologist, Eugen Fischer, had made the same assertion. The "catastrophic fall" in European fertility was bound, in his view, to "reduce considerably the number of stocks which carry on to posterity the national heritage" (Fischer, 1931, p. 105).

Negative Eugenics

The social prejudice in favor of elites found in writings on population decline was frequently turned against their supposed inferiors. The major claim here was that the "inferiority" of specified social groups was a reflection of their innate character. Left to reproduce on their own, such people would propagate their particular disability, and on account of their high fertility, they were bound to pose a serious threat to the future well-being of the entire community. It is at this point that some, but by no means all, eugenic thought took on a racist character.

Eugenics and Race

The historical experience of different countries determined whether eugenics developed primarily as a language of racial conflict or as a language of class conflict. This we can see most clearly in a brief examination of some currents in American eugenics. In the United States the legacy of slavery and the huge influx of immigrants from southern and eastern Europe who arrived in the United States during the period 1880–1914 presented problems that Europeans never had to face in the same form. It is true, though, that the European fear of the lower orders had a partial equivalence in the American anxiety over the un-American ideas and habits that aliens supposedly brought with them from an older and more degenerate world. Given the higher fertility rates among most immigrants compared to that of native Americans, fears about the future demise of the American national character were frequently expressed. Such anxieties helped launch some of the earliest work in American demography (Notestein, 1982, p. 652).

After the Russian Revolution, xenophobia and the defense of the "American way of life" took on a particularly shrill character, which was reflected in many discussions of population questions. Consider the welcoming remarks of Henry Fairfield Osborn of the American Museum of Natural History to delegates to the 1921 International Eugenics Congress. He told his audience that "in certain parts of Europe the worst elements of society have gained the ascendency and threaten the destruction of the best" (Osborn, 1923, p. 1). With proper immigration controls no such threat would materialize in America, he presumed. Many of the other delegates expressed a greater interest in the demographic and eugenic significance of the racial question in America. An exhibition was prepared for the congress, many of the displays of which presented "scientific proof" of the innate inferiority of Negroes.[1]

Such ideas were pervasive at this time, as we can judge in the remarks of an academic writer on population questions, Edward M. East of Harvard. In 1920 this scholar advanced the "theory" that

> The negro is a happy-go-lucky child, naturally expansive under simple conditions; oppressed by the restriction of civilization. He accepts his limitations; indeed he is rather glad to have them. Only when there is white blood in his veins does he cry out against the supposed injustice of his condition. (pp. 621–622)

The particular mulatto he may have had in mind was the distinguished black scholar at Harvard, W. E. B. Dubois (1920, p. 621). East seems to have been unaware that very few blacks in America were of what he called pure African stock. But to have admitted that inconvenient fact would have been to face the consequences of his own theory—the inevitability of racial protest and racial conflict.

The literature on race produced in Germany was vast and, unfortunately, is all too well known. We shall discuss below the impact on the eugenics movement of Nazi ideas on the sterilization of the unfit. In this context, though, it is important to note how many non-German writers on eugenics were imbued with strains of prejudice strikingly similar to those the Nazis were later to immortalize and thereby to discredit. In phrases that would have warmed the heart of Alfred Rosenburg, the chief Nazi race theorist, the Liverpool physician Rentoul warned of the "monstrosities" produced by racial intermarriage and of the criminal sexual appetites of the black man (1906, p. 31). Somewhat less hysterical, but also infused with prejudice and ignorance were the remarks of Caleb Saleeby that "the child of the lower races degenerates at puberty" (1921, p. 61). He followed this statement with a surre-

---

[1]See the booklet printed for the occasion, *The Second International Exhibition of Eugenics* (Baltimore, 1923, p. 108) on the less developed "brain part" of Negro skulls, and p. 120 on Negro "mental fatigue". Anti-immigrant displays were also presented.

alistic description of nonwhite cranial physiology. It is fortunate that these physicians were unlikely to encounter blacks in need of medical attention in England. In another context, Saleeby (1909) ridiculed the work of those who "would almost have us believe that the negro is mentally and morally the equal of the Caucasian" (p. xi). Julian S. Huxley held similar views. He opposed miscegenation on the grounds that society had to avoid a "large proportion of disharmonic combinations" (whatever they were; 1921, p. 21). Lucien March believed that the French faced just such a fate as a result of the immigration of "unassimilable races . . . which will furnish quickly undesirable elements," and which, because of higher fertility, will quickly spread throughout the population (1923, p. 251).

These statements are but the tip of the iceberg of racial prejudice in Europe in the period under review, and it would have been surprising if discussion of population questions developed independently of it. But in Europe, in contrast to the United States, anxiety over the future of society pointed more to questions of class than to questions of race. Consider these remarks made by a French anthropologist, Georges Vacher de Lapouge, to the 1923 International Eugenics Congress:

> The time has come when man must choose whether he will be a demigod or whether he will turn to barbarism. And this is not a figure of speech. The less well endowed classes, the residue of "uncivilizables", reproach their superiors for having created a civilization which multiplies their desires beyond the possibility of their satisfaction. An immense movement has started among races and inferior classes, and this movement which can be turned against the white race, is turned also against intellectually superior elements and against civilization itself. Class war is the real race war. (p. 6)

Eugenics and Social Class

Notions such as these were largely a reworking of nineteenth-century fears about the explosive potential of urban populations. Many writers prepared the way for eugenics by decrying the "dangerous classes" of Paris or the submerged denizens of "Outcast London" (Chevalier, 1966; Jones, 1971; Rentoul, 1906, p. xii). The development of statistical procedures in the later Victorian period made possible the measurement of this pool of apparent disorder and of many of the supposed links between fertility and social instability or racial decline. In 1906 one of Karl Pearson's associates at University College, London produced a learned study of fertility and social status, the purpose of which was to demonstrate the "very close relationship between undesirable social status and a high birth rate" (Heron, 1906, p. 21). General laborers and other "mentally and physically feebler stocks" were reproducing themselves at much greater rates than were professionals and other "abler and more capable stocks" (p. 21).

To uncover the true statistical picture of differential fertility, the superintendent of statistics for England and Wales, T. H. Stevenson, conducted a census of fertility in 1911. To help process the data, he constructed a taxonomy of social classes, from Class I (professionals) through intermediate grades to Class V (unskilled workers). Special classes were designated for agricultural laborers, miners, and textile workers, whose fertility patterns were believed to be significantly different from those of other manual workers. The results of this analysis appeared after the First World War and supported the view that poverty and high fertility were positively correlated. Although no subsequent census of fertility was conducted in Britain until after the Second World War, Stevenson's categories of social stratification, which are highly problematic, have survived to this day, as an offshoot of concern over population decline.[2]

As we have seen, before the First World War, many observers of social affairs in Britain were convinced that among the residuum of the urban poor lived many who were congenitally unfit. The Liverpool physician Rentoul was definitely not alone in his belief that people who lived in slums were predisposed hereditarily to do so (Rentoul, 1906, p. 16). Together with agricultural laborers, unskilled workers were seen as carriers of feeblemindedness, the expense of the public care of which in Poor Law institutions was a chronic source of concern among middle-class social workers and philanthropists. To some eugenicists, though, the feebleminded were "the kith and kin of the epileptic, the insane and mentally unstable, the criminal, the chronic pauper and unemployable

---

[2]See Szreter (1984) for the full story of the formulation of Stevenson's categorization of social classes.

classes," the support of whom "must impede national advance" (Tredgold, 1910, pp. 720-721).

This identification of a cluster of "degenerates" whose fertility was higher than that of the nondegenerate population character-izes many British discussions of deviance in this period. Referring again to the feebleminded, Leonard Huxley claimed in 1926 that the country could not "preserve and multiply these weaklings in mind who make the nation incurably below C-3", that is, below the minimum standard for induction into the Army (p. 38). Public assistance of any kind, Leonard Darwin (1917) wrote, while soothing to humanitarian sentiment, was dysgenic. The strength of such "civilizing influences" in the past helped to "explain why ancient civilizations have often died out" (p. 62). At the height of the world economic crisis, R. Ruggles Gates, a noted botanist, told the Centenary Meeting of the British Association that public fi-nancial support for working-class nutrition and health was not in the national interest. "The view that populations exist as blind mouths to be fed and educated regardless of their racial worth," he argued, "is all too prevalent and will lead us along the road to racial decay" (Gates, 1932a, p. 307; see also his article in the same source for his indictment of the wastefulness of social welfare pro-vision).

As we have already seen in Chapter 2, the themes of urban de-generacy and hereditary insanity were prominent in turn-of-the-century French literature, such as in the novels of Zola and the works of Brieux and of other French writers. These concerns were at the heart of the eugenics movement, which in France had a par-ticularly wide appeal among scientists still wedded to the Lamarck-ian tradition. It is this feature of their thought that separates much French eugenic writing from the more radical positions of men like Vacher de Lapouge. For a Lamarckian, the deprivation of pov-erty, like the "taint" of alcoholism, tuberculosis, or venereal dis-ease, could be passed on to the offspring of the poor or diseased. But there was an inherent optimism in this position, since the re-moval of the children of the poor to a rural environment or the improvement in urban conditions that produced their "degener-acy" would suffice virtually immediately to cure it (Schneider, 1982, passim).

For this reason, and because of the hostility of the Catholic

Church to interference with reproduction, relatively few French eugenicists went to the extremes of Vacher de Lapouge, whose curious mixture of antisemitism, anthropology, and anarchism would have been more at home in a Nazi institute of race hygiene than in a quiet French provincial university. (For a survey of the ideas of Vacher de Lapouge, see Guiral, 1977, pp. 34–47, and Lapouge, 1899.) There were some echoes of his work in the writings of René Martial, a medical anthropologist in the faculty of medicine in Paris in the 1930s, who explicitly linked the problem of degeneracy to the decline in the birth rate. He told Parisian medical students in 1938 that, since fecundity is proportional to the purity of the race and the stability of "local crossings" (Martial, 1938, p. 123), immigration and even interregional intermarriage had to be stopped. Here was an ingenious explanation of the decline of French fertility. Like his British counterparts, but long after many of them had begun to feel embarrassed about the proximity of their ideas to those of the Nazis, Martial also advocated the sterilization of epileptics, alcoholics, and the mentally ill (Martial, 1939, pp. 249, 251, 290; see also Martial, 1938).

In Germany, eugenics became part of a cult of race improvement and race mysticism institutionalized after the Nazi seizure of power in 1933. Jews were stigmatized as social pariahs from the moment Hitler took over as chancellor, but it is important to remember that many non-Jewish Germans suffering from disabilities or diseases deemed hereditary were also placed at risk by Hitler's political success. Well before the "final solution of the Jewish problem" had emerged from the dark recesses of the Nazi High Command, much discussion and planning took place about the need for compulsory sterilization, and later for the euthanasia, of the undesirable and the unfit.

Interest in the subject of genetic hygiene or "race improvement" antedated the creation of the National Socialist party. In 1904 the *Journal of Racial and Social Biology* was founded. Its editor, Alfred Ploetz, was also the founder of the Society for Racial Hygiene, which was modeled after the English Eugenics Education Society. He became prominent in this field in part because of his entry in an essay contest sponsored by Alfred Krupp on the question, "What can we learn from the principles of Darwinism for application to domestic political development of the laws of the state?"

Over the years, he and his journal propagated eugenic ideas supporting the sterilization of the unfit. It should cause no surprise to learn that he and other leading German social biologists joined the Nazi party and worked to enact the law of 28 June 1933 for the sterilization of those bearing hereditary disease. It is in the context of this legislation that we must place the praise of the elderly Karl Pearson, the great statistician and eugenicist, for Hitler's effort to rebuild the German nation (Mosse, 1978, pp. 76–93).

The legislation of 1933, followed by the Nuremburg laws and other pieces of Nazi policy, caused a breach in the international eugenics movement from which it never recovered. In the report of the conference of international eugenic organizations, which met in Zurich in 1934, we can see the extent to which eugenicists drew back from negative eugenics as practiced by the Nazis. The major discussion centered around the new sterilization laws, which to some delegates from France and the Low Countries seemed to violate the humanitarianism that they believed was at the heart of eugenics. For example, to sterilize those who suffered from Huntington's chorea would eliminate both their offspring who would have had the disease and those who would have been free of it. To some delegates, this approximated a massacre of the innocents, which was intrinsically objectionable, but doubly so at a time of "diminishing natality."

The German delegates, of course, would have none of this. Falk Ruttke, director of the committee of public health of the Ministry of the Interior, insisted that "everything which can be harmful to the future of the German people must be extirpated by force" (Schreiber, 1935, p. 87). Dr. Arthur Gutt, director of the Ministry of the Interior, explained the new legislation to the delegates, and Dr. Karl Astel provided statistics relating to compulsory sterilization in Thuringia. In that one area alone, encompassing a population of 1.6 million people, 1234 compulsory sterilizations took place between 1 January and 1 July 1934 (Schreiber, 1935, pp. 78–92).

Many eugenicists were not averse to considering the case for voluntary sterilization of people with hereditary diseases. But most of those associated with eugenics in Britain and France were deeply troubled by Nazi racial policies, which, they realized, exposed the darker side of their movement. To many eugenicists, German developments meant the parting of the ways. One meeting of the International Union for the Scientific Study of Population, founded in 1930 by the American demographer Raymond Pearl and the Italian demographer Corrado Gini, was moved from Rome to London to prevent Gini from exploiting it as propaganda for fascism. For similar reasons, American demographers boycotted another meeting of the organization held in Berlin (Notestein, 1982, p. 674).

Indeed, even the term *eugenics* came to carry unsavory connotations in the period of the Second World War and after. This was as true in the United States as it was elsewhere. It is important to note, though, that in 1933, legislation permitting the sterilization of the unfit was on the statute books of 30 states of the Union, and that over 8000 people were sterilized in the years 1928–1933 alone (Schreiber, 1935, pp. 83–84). If Hitler can be said to have accomplished anything, it was to undermine the concept of race improvement that underlay these and many similar measures adopted in a number of countries in the period 1900–1933.

The fact that some eugenicists wound up as fellow travelers of the Nazis should not lead us to conclude that eugenics was a proto-fascist movement. It is better to see eugenics as a movement of middle-class professionals and men of property who found a biological language to express their fears of revolution or proletarianization, either of which constituted in their eyes the degeneration of the race. This is why the eugenicist and Oxford philosopher F. C. S. Schiller openly expressed his sympathies with fascism, as the most effective antisocialist weapon. Socialism to him was "an unintelligent attempt to equalize human conditions without regard to mind or capacity, which is inspired mainly by envy and sentimentalism" (Schiller, 1932, p. 8; see also, Abel, 1955, pp. 146–147).

At least on the question of socialism and on the need to improve the quality of the race, fascism seemed to be speaking sense to many eugenicists. In addition, many Catholics, while vigorously opposing eugenic ideas in any form, still found attractive the pronatalist attitudes of virtually all fascist leaders. Furthermore, Mussolini's Italy and Franco's Spain had granted an honored place to the church which, after the Russian Revolution and the Spanish Civil War, had to face what conservatives saw as a ferocious onslaught from the atheistic armies of the left. To those whose Catholicism underpinned both their conservatism and their pronatalism, perhaps all was not evil in the fascist camp. Halliday Sutherland, whose early medical practice had begun in Spain in 1908, was invited back by the Franco government in 1946. By then he was a well-known crusader against contraception. His account of his visit included a defense of Franco and a sympathetic appraisal of the ideology of Antonio Primo de Rivera, the founder of the Falangist movement (Sutherland, 1936, pp. 235-236; 1947, pp. 83, 92-93). The fascist "solution" to problems of internal social instability clearly had an appeal to many exponents of the fear of population decline.

SOCIAL DEMOCRACY AND POPULATION DECLINE

What is more surprising is how widely shared by the left was concern about population decline in Europe in this period. What could socialists and reforming liberals have had in common with the views of conservative eugenicists such as Dr. C. M. Burns, who in a book on infant and maternal mortality, called for a reduction of "the flotsam in future generations" not by environmental improvement but by better breeding? After all, she noted, "The black spot cannot be 'bred out' of a terrier's litter by merely giving the mother a good kennel" (Burns, 1942, p. 246). It is obvious that this sort of negative eugenics was repugnant to men and women of the left, many of whom were nonetheless prepared to argue that aggregate population growth had to be kept up in order to assure the future of social democracy in Europe.

Catholic socialists on the continent had no difficulty in reconciling their pronatalism with their commitment to the liberation of the working class from the fetters of unbridled capitalism. Many followed Marx in excoriating Malthus as the pessimistic ideologist of the selfish bourgeoisie, a man who blamed the poor for their poverty and opposed state welfare as counterproductive. This is one of the themes of the scholarly work of the Italian radical politician and economist, Francesco S. Nitti, who later became prime minister after the First World War and received a Nobel Peace Prize for his work on behalf of the League of Nations. In a book published in 1893 and translated into French, German, and English on

Population and the Social System, he developed the idea that a socialist society would be one with a fertility rate higher than that of a capitalist society, because socialism grew out of a commitment to collective rather than individual morality. This view was based on the assertion "that every system of morality which leads to individualism is contrary to a great fecundity of race, and that, on the other hand, every system of morality, which has as a fundamental principal social solidarity and mutual assistance is favourable to a large birth rate" (Nitti, 1894, p. 124). We have already cited (Chapter 2) similar pronatalist sentiments of French commentators of Republican sympathies, such as Arsène Dumont and Émile Zola. Their writing contributed to a wide body of opinion on the European left that decried a slowdown in rates of population growth as a reflection of the decadence of capitalism.

Others saw a decline in fertility as an obstacle to social reform. One of the most influential figures in the field of social administration in Britain was the socialist academic Richard Titmuss. In a book written jointly with Kathleen Titmuss, we may find one version of this argument. They asserted in 1942 that a slow-growing population is more interested in security than in reform. A declining rate of population growth, therefore, meant that "society will lose the mental attitude that is essential for social progress." They admitted that an aging population was one "ripe [in] experience and Victorian memories," but added these rhetorical questions: "Are these the gifts we require to build a New Social Order? If this age structure explains in part our shortcomings during the past ten years, will it not also shape our future; a cautious, timid, benevolent" future, perhaps, but not a socialist future (Titmuss and Titmuss, 1942, p. 47)?

The Titmusses formulated a second aspect of the socialist analysis of population decline. On the assumption that "man's attitude to the reproduction of his own species is the key to all other problems" (Titmuss and Titmuss, 1942, p. 31), they concluded that declining fertility was an indictment of capitalism on the part of people who did not want to bring children into the world it had created. The ethical socialism of R. H. Tawney is writ large in the view that "so long as men, twisting, turning, fighting, and rolling in an economic society, in which they are saturated with class thinking, are forced to compete one with another, so long will they refuse to reproduce themselves" (Titmuss and Titmuss, 1942, p. 116).

The social biologist Lancelot Hogben, who like Titmuss and Tawney taught at the London School of Economics, concurred. "The population crisis to which urban civilization is now heading," he wrote in 1936, "is the biological proof of its inadequacy" (Hogben, 1936, p. 50). Enid Charles, the author of *The Menace of Underpopulation*, and Hogben's wife, wrote similarly that the "ultimate condemnation" of capitalism "is that it has now ceased to be able to accommodate the biological machinery by which any form of society can be perpetuated" (1936, p. 223). The assumption of many of these writers, with the exception of the iconoclastic and agnostic Hogben, was that a socialist society would be, by definition, a more fertile one.

Liberal economists avoided similar indictments of capitalism, but many of them were worried about the consequences of the slowdown of population growth rates. J. A. Hobson, a member of the National Birth-rate Commission, found the discussion of population decline to be perfectly compatible with his underconsumptionist theories (Marchant, 1920b). John Maynard Keynes, in the late 1930s, advanced the view that a recovery of fertility rates would help stimulate aggregate demand and replenish sources of capital (Keynes, 1937, pp. 13–17). Sir William Beveridge, his biographer tells us, derived his concern about the question of fertility from three sources:

> firstly, from a fear of the ultimate collapse of the most "advanced" races; secondly, from a desire to avoid producing a society over-loaded with old people; and thirdly, from a belief that birth control was mainly practiced by the most "responsible" sections of society and might therefore be harming the "national stock". (Harris, 1977, p. 342)

These sentiments were enshrined in the Beveridge Report of 1942, out of which came much of the momentum leading to the social reforms of the later 1940s. Therein maternal welfare provision and family allowances were defended on the grounds that women "have vital work to do in insuring the adequate continuance of the British race and British ideals in the world (Report on Social Insurance and Allied Services, p. 53).

Beveridge's ideas on population questions bring out many of the reasons why social reformers' fears of population decline resembled those of their political enemies. First, let us take two of the most prominent exponents of these views, Beveridge, the Liberal, and Sidney Webb, the Fabian bureaucrat par excellence. Both were strongly influenced both by positivism and by the social biology of Francis Galton. To them fertility was a social fact whose laws could be ascertained by appropriate study. The science of population dynamics was bound to have an attraction for them, as it did for commentators of very different political views. Second, Beveridge and Webb epitomized in their work and thought a form of bureaucratic collectivism that coincided at many points. To those who shared their administrative cast of mind, fertility was but one aspect of human behavior that, like most others, could be and ought to be regulated in the national interest. Third, Webb's form of Fabianism was the doctrine of professional men and women who had relatively little direct contact with the working class, and who at times expressed strong disapproval of the "residuum," as an excrescence that had to be swept away. Both Webb, the Fabian, and Beveridge, the Liberal, believed that "The 'survival of the fittest' in an environment unfavourable to progress may . . . mean the survival of the lowest parasite" (Webb, 1910, pp. 235–237 as cited in Freeden, 1979, p. 647). Consequently, Webb claimed that "it is our business, as eugenists, deliberately to manipulate the environment so that the survivors may be of the type which we regard as the highest" (p. 647).

Fourth, both Beveridge and Webb were consummate opportunists who used the specter of population decline to inspire or frighten politicians who needed a reason to set reforms in motion. A mixture of philanthropy and patriotism, fueled by concern over population growth, did much to advance the cause of welfare legislation in Western Europe in this century. In Sweden many policy initiatives in the 1930s and after grew out of the commitment stated by Alva Myrdal in 1941: "When the population fails to regenerate itself, the problem of how the human material may be preserved and improved becomes urgent" (Kalvemark, 1980, p. 16).[3] In campaigns on behalf of infant and maternal health in both France and Britain, we can see the co-mingling of strange bedfellows whose

[3]We are grateful to Dr. Philip Ogden for drawing this reference to our attention.

only idea in common was anxiety over fertility limitation. Similarly, the call for free education in the interwar years in Britain was backed up by the argument that high educational costs for parents were in large part responsible for "the toll . . . which is at present extracted from our birth-rate" (Leybourne and White, 1940, p. 324). Demographic arguments once again came in handy in struggles for social reform.

Finally, the social democratic advocacy of the fear of population decline makes sense as an expression of the deep patriotism of the Western European left. The national consciousness of the French left drew on the tradition of the *levée en masse* (call to arms) of the revolutionary and Napoleonic periods and of the heroic resistance of the Paris Commune to enemies foreign and domestic. The force of *union sacrée* was felt in the surge of mass enthusiasm for war in August 1914. In Britain the call for the defense of King and Country drew the same overwhelming response.

Working-class patriotism did not abate in the interwar years. In this period, too, it was with some justification that socialists in Britain identified the future of their cause with the future of their nation. Since social democracy had collapsed everywhere else in Europe between 1919 and 1940, its existence would be assured, many believed, only if Britain remained healthy and secure. For this reason, men and women on the left believed they had cause for concern over declining rates of population growth that were, in their view, incompatible with national vitality and, if continued, a threat to national survival itself.

Population Dynamics and Policies, 1945–1964   4

POLITICAL AND ECONOMIC CHANGE
AFTER THE SECOND WORLD WAR

We have seen that there are really two aspects of the fear of population decline that were expressed between 1870 and 1940. The first concerns general fertility levels; the second concerns variations in the fertility levels of specific social groups. After the Second World War, both fears receded, and concerns over differential fertility were largely discredited. The recognition of the consequences of applying racial theories to the "final solution of the Jewish problem" made it impossible in civilized discourse to use the language of animal breeding so prevalent in population debate earlier in the century.

The war transformed the political and intellectual atmosphere in which population questions were discussed. Burdened with the legacy of collaboration, the radical right was eclipsed for a time, and into obscurity with it went much of the chauvinistic advocacy of natality on military or class lines. Bolstered by the crucial role played in the resistance to Hitler by communists and socialists, the left gained ground and won the support of many who simply had no wish to return to the social conditions of the conservative-dominated world of the 1930s. A revised and updated Christian Democracy, purged of its more extreme elements, came to terms with organized labor and state intervention. American influences helped spread the gospel of pure environmentalism as an alternative to pure heredity as a source of social problems and social progress. In effect, as the conditions changed, so the language of class conflict changed with them.

In consequence, there were few echoes after 1945 of the need to

sterilize the unfit, the undesirable, or the unemployed, or to maximize the fertility of elites. In addition, the advocates of the view
that wealth and innate ability were linked genetically never recovered from the shock of the Great Depression. In the period surrounding the Second World War, many supporters of measures to
change the social balance of fertility abandoned their earlier views.
Others retained them but lapsed into uncomfortable silence.

Their silence can also be traced to the fact that even before the
war many of the scientific arguments used to justify the restriction
of the fertility of certain classes had been rejected by scientists
themselves. Once the inheritance of diseases via carriers (whose
genes contained recessive traits not expressed in their own biology) was firmly established, the idea of eliminating what were
deemed hereditary diseases by the sterilization of those who suffered from them was shown to be dangerous nonsense. Furthermore, advances in pathology, psychiatry, and epidemiology
precluded the perpetuation of many early claims of heritability for
certain diseases, such as tuberculosis or certain neurotic conditions, or arguments that such diseases were merely symptoms of
"damaged germ plasm." Similarly, advances in the study of mu-
tations cast doubt on the validity of theories of the survival of the
fittest imbedded in social Darwinian rhetoric (Hogben, 1934, pp.
25-26; Muller, 1936, p. 56).

With some justification, biologists such as Lancelot Hogben ridiculed those worried about the proliferating unfit, not because of
their emphasis on the importance of genetic research, but because
of their profound ignorance of the supposed scientific basis of their
views (1931, pp. 99, 209, 211). The advocates of eugenic doctrine
could not easily dismiss the opinion of scientists who argued con-
vincingly that, before we could know whether human attributes
or abilities were inherited (and if so, to what degree), social conditions would have to be equalized (Haldane, 1938, p. 112). The
essential problem of eugenics was that biology had largely passed
it by.

Furthermore, the fact that the postwar baby boom lasted longer
than anyone had predicted made it seem that somehow all the fuss
over low fertility had achieved results and that therefore old war-
riors could rest content. Had gross reproduction rates in the mid-

1950s been as low as those of the mid-1930s, it is likely that the fear of aggregate population decline would have continued to plague discussions of social policy. But until the late 1960s, such was not the case.

While the main reason for the eclipse of interwar worries about low fertility was this recovery of the birth rate, the discontinuity between the prewar and postwar periods can be seen as clearly in the economic realm as in the world of political and scientific ideas. Indeed, the post-1945 years form one of the most remarkable chapters in Western economic history.

The sheer speed at the rebuilding of Europe after 1945 was astounding. In part, economic reconstruction was a result of the injection of huge amounts of American capital in the late 1940s when the German economy was still prostrate. In part, it was a reflection of the vast store of human capital in Europe—the knowledge, skills, and services of millions of people who began constructive tasks after the war. Of equal importance was the creation of a set of economic and political arrangements that brought the stability essential to the revival of manufacture, finance, and commerce. The International Monetary Fund was set up to act as a lender of last resort in international trade. American-sponsored moves toward the political integration of Europe were rejected by European leaders, but a framework for economic cooperation was fashioned along the lines of the Monet plan, out of which the Common Market was born. In addition, high levels of domestic consumption were stimulated by the adoption of tools of economic analysis and policies associated with John Maynard Keynes. His approach was particularly useful at a time when a capital investment boom was long overdue. What he offered was a path to economic growth not littered by the wreckage of battles between Capital and Labor.

The optimistic belief that many of the conflicts and concepts of the prewar years had faded from the scene had other major political expressions. The creation of the United Nations embodied a belief, naive perhaps but certainly widely expressed, that the Grand Alliance against the Nazis had made it possible to outlaw war. American isolationism had rendered the League of Nations stillborn after the First World War, but a change in American attitudes by 1945 made it appear that the United Nations could become an effective peacekeeping body, so conspicuous by its absence between 1919 and 1939.

Within Europe, domestic developments also seemed to describe a clear break with the status quo antebellum. The election by a landslide of a Labour government in Britain and the rebirth of Social Democracy throughout Western Europe after the Nazi occupation of the continent changed the political environment in which social policy was formulated and enacted. Despite the heavy burdens of indebtedness imposed on European nations by the war, there emerged throughout the continent a major extension of social provision and a commitment to the maintenance of full employment, whatever the cost. Those commitments would not go unchallenged indefinitely, but in the immediate postwar years they described a consensus in Europe that simply had not existed before 1939.

It is highly unlikely that the birth rate surge of the immediate postwar period was prompted by these social reforms. As had happened after 1918, a wave of deferred births followed the end of the Second World War. But the most striking feature of the post-1945 decade, which distinguished it clearly from earlier years, was the persistence of at least somewhat higher fertility even after the period of adjustment to postwar conditions.

Higher fertility put in a different and less glaring light steps taken in the immediate postwar years to broaden demographic research and increase the information on population questions available to politicians and bureaucrats. It is ironic that the Royal Commission on Population, established in Britain in 1944 to investigate the problem of a society with low fertility, reported its findings in 1949, when the birth rate was higher than it had been at any time in the interwar period.

Other postwar developments of academic demography also reflected prewar concerns. In 1947 the prewar Population Investigation Committee, established in London in 1935, launched its periodical, *Population Studies*, then (and still) the only British journal devoted to the study of the subject. In 1946 the French journal *Population* made its first appearance. Then and in the intervening years it had served as the organ of the influential official body, the

Institut National d'Études Démographiques (INED). The review *Économie et Statistique* is the product of the Institut National de la Statistique et des Études Économiques, established in 1945 and yet another manifestation of prewar ideas that appeared in a fundamentally different environment.

Of course, no one in the late 1940s could have known that the postwar recovery of fertility (or indeed the boom in world trade) would continue for another two decades. After all, there had also been an uneven but real postwar boom after the 1914–1918 war, but it was short-lived and was followed shortly by the onset of mass unemployment. Still, by the early 1950s, it was clear to all but the most cautious observers that the dismal world of the 1930s was indeed dead and that a period of relative prosperity had begun.

The most important stability condition that made this possible was in the realm of international politics. Despite the tension over Berlin, the atomic bomb, and the Korean War, most people on both sides of the Iron Curtain accepted that the demarcation of spheres of influence between the United States and the Soviet Union was here to stay. In addition, the end of what had seemed ineradicable conflicts between the victorious and the defeated nations—France and Germany, Yugoslavia and Italy, the United States and Japan—presaged a period of cooperation in reconstruction and development.

Meanwhile, the systematic exploitation of cheap energy sources helped fuel the expansion of the Western economy and stimulate the process of industrialization in the non-European world. In the postwar decades, more efficient and more centralized industrial enterprises forged working relationships with labor and the state, which had been foreshadowed in the 1930s but not realized before the Second World War. One important consequence of these changes was a major improvement in wage levels. Due to agricultural expansion and the steady growth in world trade, rising real wages and nutritional levels were registered in both Europe and the United States.

It is the unparalleled prosperity of the period between the early 1950s and early 1970s that is the appropriate context in which to set both demographic developments and the apparent subsidence of the fear of population decline.

THE BABY BOOM

The Resurgence of Fertility

In a number of countries, the post-1945 baby boom was one of the most dramatic demographic shifts in recent history. In the United States, fertility rose by over two-thirds, from the record-low fertility levels of the 1930s to levels in the last half of the 1950s approaching those of the period 1905–1910 (U.S. Bureau of the Census, 1975, Table B-3136). However, it is important to understand that this baby boom in its complete form characterized only a few of the industrialized countries, albeit also some of the largest. The four countries that experienced the most substantial and longest-lasting boom were all English-speaking former dependencies of Great Britain: the United States, Canada, Australia and New Zealand (Teitelbaum, 1973, p. 653).

The fertility increases recorded in these true baby boom countries were substantial and were sustained throughout the 1950s and well into the 1960s. In the United States, for example, the period total fertility rate rose from its Great Depression low of 2.2 in 1936 to a high of nearly 3.8 in 1957. It was not until 1972 that fertility below 2.2 was seen once again. Figure 4.1 shows the course of period fertility in this first group of four Western countries.

The countries of Western Europe, as well as some in Eastern Europe, also registered a postwar increase in fertility. However, in contrast to the sustained booms of the above four countries, most of these could be fairly described as "boomlets," that is, rising trends in both the late 1940s and later in the 1950s, deriving partly from realization of deferred births and a surge in marriage, but which never reached the levels of true baby boom countries. As may be seen in Figures 4.2–4.7, most of the countries in this group had already had fertility levels at or near replacement by the 1930s. The end of the Second World War was followed by a brief baby boomlet that appears as a 3- to 4-year "spike" in the graph, followed by fully two decades of relatively unchanging fertility levels in the general range of 2.0 to 3.0. The superimposition of the U.S. fertility pattern in Figures 4.2–4.5 is a graphic demonstration of the sharp differences in postwar fertility experience between the first (true baby boom) and the second (boomlet) group of Western countries.

Finally, the third grouping of industrialized countries (Figure 4.6–4.7), consisting of Eastern Europe and Japan, showed more varied and sometimes erratic fertility patterns. Some (e.g., Czechoslovakia, and probably what is now East Germany) recorded fertility levels in the 1930s as low as those prevailing in Western Europe, followed by a postwar baby boomlet and subsequent decline. Others (e.g., Japan, Poland, and the Soviet Union) did not register low fertility in the 1930s but saw substantial declines in the 1950s after a short-lived postwar baby boomlet. Many Eastern European countries experienced below-replacement fertility in the 1960s, and several undertook pronatalist policies of which the most dramatic results were seen in Rumania.

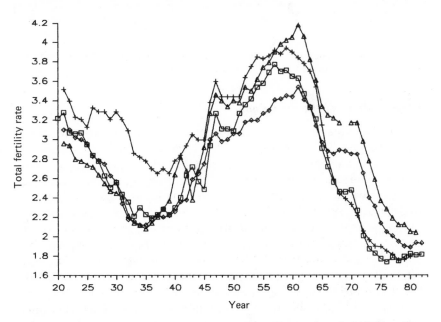

Figure 4.1 Total fertility rates, 1920–1983, for Australia (◊), Canada (+), New Zealand (△), and the United States (□). Source: See Appendix A.

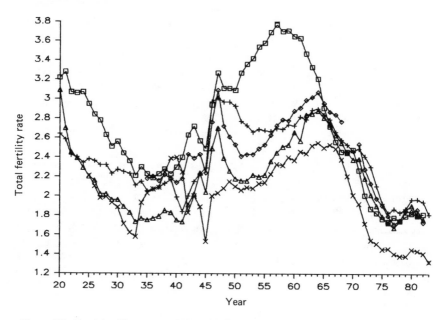

Figure 4.2 Total fertility rates, 1920–1983, for England and Wales (△), France (+), Scotland (◇), the United States (□), and West Germany (×).

Interpretations of the Baby Boom

Various explanations have been offered to account for the striking demographic phenomenon of the baby boom. One school of opinion holds that the fertility experience of the postwar decades was an aberration arising from the "random shocks" of wartime and postwar developments, and not a fundamental departure from prewar trends. The baby boom is thus an oddity, of significance to policymakers no doubt, but of little importance in the longer-term history of population change. Some saw a parallel between the post-1918 baby boom and that following the Second World War. Since the former gave way to then-record interwar low fertility rates within a short period of time, it was logical to believe that the same pattern would prevail once the repercussions of the 1939–1945 war had passed.

The problem remained, though, that the arrival of postponed births after 1945 constituted only the beginning of the surge in

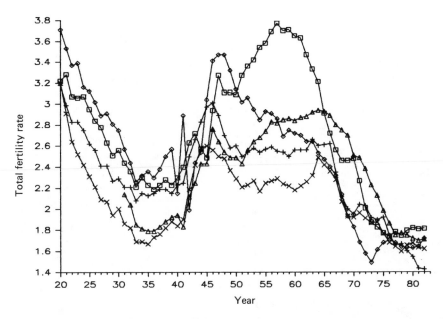

Figure 4.3 Total fertility rates, 1920–1983, for Denmark (+), Finland (◊), Norway (△), Sweden (×), and the United States (□).

postwar births. What could not be explained solely by reference to the war experience was why the prewar decline in fertility was arrested and in a number of cases dramatically reversed over a 20-year period.

Much of the theoretical and empirical debate over the meaning of the postwar baby boom surrounds the American case. It is well established that the sharp increases in U.S. fertility derived principally from two major changes in behavior: (1) the shift toward earlier and more nearly universal marriage; and (2) a larger proportion of women having at least two children. While there were increases as well in the number of families with three or four children, the number of very large families (i.e., five or more children) actually declined (Ryder, 1982, pp. 286–292).

Proposed explanations have included changes in sociocultural norms surrounding childbearing, social-psychological effects of growing up during the Great Depression, and the effects of economic change between the 1930s and 1950s (Bean, 1983, pp.

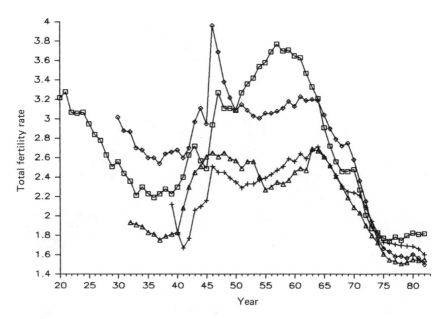

Figure 4.4 Total fertility rates, 1920–1983, for Belgium (+), the Netherlands (◊), Switzerland (△), and the United States (□).

353–365). Among these explanations, one of the more prominent is that developed by the American economist Richard Easterlin. His central argument is that the baby boom was a generational phenomenon. The generations of childbearing age in the postwar period were born in the 1920s and 1930s, when fertility reached record lows. As a result, these were small cohorts that, despite the trials of the depression and Second World War during their childhood and adolescent years, experienced only limited competition for the available educational and occupational slots. Hence, in Easterlin's view, these generations experienced relatively high achievement and earnings (relative to their older peers), and hence had an optimistic view of the future that stimulated earlier marriage and higher fertility.

Easterlin's hypothesis is based on the central assumption that adult aspirations are formed in adolescence by people living in parental households. Young married adults, he argued, develop a sense of "relative income," that is, the way they see their own

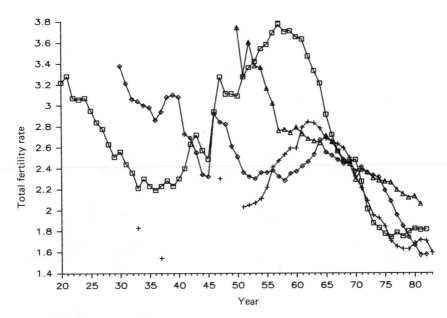

Figure 4.5 Total fertility rates, 1920–1983, for Austria (+), Italy (◇), the United States (□), and Yugoslavia (△).

expected earnings compared with their parents' earnings. When their relative income rises, they will be prepared to have more children. Such was the case in the period of economic expansion in the 1950s, when aspirations formed in the previous generation of austerity and warfare were realized or exceeded by a substantial part of the population.

In contrast, when young married adults perceive a fall in relative income, as this age group did in the late 1960s and 1970s, young couples will tend to restrict their fertility. Such declines in relative income can result from the maturation of large birth cohorts, as when the children of the baby boom entered a labor market tightening because of abundant labor supply (Easterlin, 1976, pp. 417–425). While based largely on American data, Easterlin's work has also provided a framework for the analysis of European and extra-European demographic trends in the post-1945 period (Ermish, 1982, pp. 141–155).

An alternative economic interpretation has been developed by

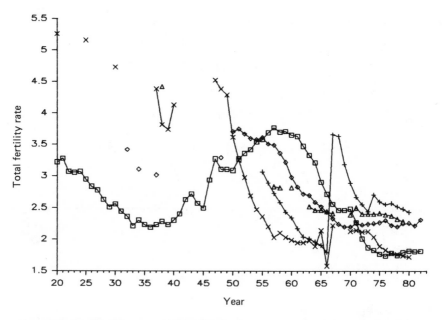

Figure 4.6 Total fertility rates, 1920–1983, for Japan (×), Poland (◊), Rumania (+), the Soviet Union (△), and the United States (□).

the American economist Gary Becker, again on the basis of American data (Becker, 1960, pp. 209–231). What is termed (with tongue firmly in cheek) the "new home economics" approach is, in effect, an argument about the opportunity costs of childbearing as the key variable in fertility swings. Thus, in the late 1940s and 1950s, the end of the war and demobilization of several million soldiers led to a drop in demand for female labor and a consequent decline in relative wages for women. This served to reduce the potential income forgone by women choosing to stay at home and raise children rather than to go out to work. It was, therefore, a perfectly rational economic choice for couples to "arrange" their labor resources around larger families rather than for both husband and wife to seek full-time employment. By the mid-1960s, the argument proceeds, the situation had been reversed. Increased demand for female labor raised the absolute and relative rewards of work and thereby raised the opportunity costs of maternity. The result was a substantial decline in fertility.

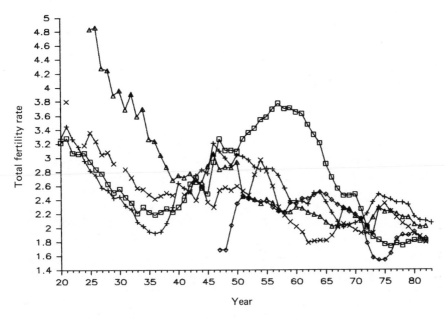

Figure 4.7 Total fertility rates, 1920–1983, for Bulgaria ($\triangle$), Czechoslovakia (+), East Germany ($\diamond$), and the United States ($\square$).

A similar view has long been influential in studies of historical demography, in particular, in the interpretation of the decline of fertility in Europe after 1870 (Banks, 1954). More recently, there are signs that the new home economics is less an alternative to Easterlin's hypothesis than a complementary approach to a multifaceted problem (Sanderson, 1976, pp. 469–477). It is clear, too, that the variety of European fertility patterns in the post-1945 period requires an explanation that goes beyond a simple application of the fruits of American-based research to the European (and extra-European) experience.

Policy Developments in the Postwar Years

Whatever the real sources of fertility fluctuations, it is apparent that social policies were formulated after 1945 in a context of uncertainty about whether the postwar surge in fertility would last. We have already referred to the analogy contemporaries drew with the post-1918 baby boom; clearly, it would have been unwise for policymakers to rule out the possibility that history would repeat itself after 1945. It did not, but the anticipation that it would, coupled with the long experience of low fertility, helps to explain why the nervousness about population decline, which had been such a salient feature of prewar demographic discussions, lasted well into the postwar period.

As we have seen, the resurgence of Social Democracy in Europe in the wake of the defeat of Hitler provided advocates of welfare provision with a political mandate and an opportunity they had never had before, and are unlikely to have again. It is not surprising, therefore, that it became impossible in postwar Europe to differentiate between those who advocated state support for childbearing as a measure of redistributive justice and those who pressed for the same measures for pronatalist reasons. For example, the case for the establishment of a complete maternity service in Britain was presented jointly by groups and individuals who came out of the old, prewar eugenics movement and by others whose political commitments were closer to those of the Labour government (Population Investigation Committee, 1948; see also Wallach, 1983).

There is a similar fusion of alternative visions of population policy in the post-1945 development of child psychology and child psychiatry. The work of John Bowlby and others associated with the Tavistock Institute in London presented striking evidence of the damage arguably done to infants whose mothers had been unable to look after them in the first years of their lives. The implication was clearly that women's participation in the labor market had potentially harmful psychologial effects for their offspring.

While some feminists have taken this development to be part of a deliberate attempt to force women back to the home after the active years of the Second World War, it was not the intention of Bowlby and his colleagues to provide a medical justification for the cult of domesticity (Riley, 1983). Nor can it be argued that the vulgarizers of psychiatry in the United States and Europe were sufficiently influential to persuade women to stay at home and thereby to raise larger families. It is true, though, that anyone committed to family policy on pronatalist lines would welcome a set of theories that threw considerable light on the putative psychological costs to the family of labor-force participation by married women with young children.

Whatever the outlook or motivation of policymakers in the postwar period, there was little doubt that, in the true baby boom countries, educational provision had to be expanded to be able to cope with the substantial increase in cohorts of school-entry age. This demographic pressure on the number of schools, allied to a teacher shortage, ensured a dramatic bolstering of the American educational system. This was made an urgent national priority in 1957, when the Soviet Union launched its first satellite, Sputnik. The apparent Soviet lead in technology seemed to many to be traceable to deficiencies in the educational system, and in particular, to the way American schoolchildren were introduced to science and technology. A major program of federal support for education was launched in 1958 in the revealingly named National Defense Education Act.

Educational policy in Europe reflected the more pressing tasks of clearing away the rubble of war and rebuilding the social infrastructure of countries torn apart by occupation, collaboration, resistance, and combat. The relatively minor character of the surge in fertility, compared to that of the United States, also meant that the specifically demographic pressure on educational provision was less severe in Britain and Western Europe.

Where European policy initiatives departed sharply from American legislation was in the field of family allowances and subsidies. This in part reflected the relative remoteness of the American federal government from the formulation of welfare policy concerning the costs of childbearing, and in part it was due to the special character of the American baby boom. But more importantly, the European developments in this field reflected the new welfare consensus shared by Social Democrats and Christian Democrats alike.

The French signaled their commitment to a comprehensive approach to family policy by setting up a High Consultative Committee on Population and the Family as a constituent part of the first postwar provisional government. This agency was to advise government departments on all demographic issues, and as we have noted above, the INED was the body it created for the gathering and analysis of population trends. But although it became the practice to appoint a minister of population (usually the minister of health) as the authority responsible for coordinating public measures related to the family, population, and immigration, this post never had the funding or political weight to set its stamp on a coherent and integrated governmental policy. For example, family allowances were distributed by the Division of Social Security of the Ministry of Labor, and family policy was in the ambit of the Division of Social Welfare of the Ministry of Health (McIntosh, 1983, pp. 105, 120–121). This fragmentation of political authority may help to explain why the initial impulse to provide family assistance and allowances faded rapidly in the 1950s and 1960s. Of course, the baby boomlet itself induced a degree of complacency about the responsibility of the state to encourage high fertility (Huss, 1981).

The postwar baby boomlet also changed the context in which French discussions of immigration took place. In the postwar period, immigration was welcomed as an aid to the demographic recovery of France. But it was soon recognized that immigrants tend to adopt the fertility regime of their "host" populations. Thus immigrant labor was of importance in the development of the French economy, but with the revival of native French fertility, there was no intrinsically demographic reason for adopting a pro-immigration line. Over time, hostility to North African-born Frenchmen or to their French-born children grew, and echoes were heard of some of the racialistic rhetoric used in prewar discussions of immigration. Ironically, this recrudescence of the French concern about immigration may be due to the recognition that her old rivalry with Germany was at last over, and that if there was a threat to France, it was that of inundation by the Maghreb—Algeria, Morocco, and Tunisia (McIntosh, 1983, p. 99).

The explosive nature of such issues in the German political context is obvious. Here lies the source of much of the reticence of German politicians about population trends, and their relative backwardness in the field of population research and policy. The shadow of the Nazi period still makes discussion of such issues fraught with difficulty. The pronatalist assumptions of National Socialism led the first postwar governments to define their role in family policy as essentially neutral. Family allowances and tax relief were provided but primarily with the aim of remedying the economic inequalities that arise from the burdens of bearing and raising children. Some initiatives were taken by the newly formed Ministry for the Family in 1957, but on the whole, the operative assumption was that the private sector—voluntary organizations and church groups—would provide child care and other family-support facilities. There was, however, some continuity with the Nazi period in terms of the maintenance of anticontraceptive laws and attitudes, in particular within the medical profession, but again the Nazi past made it difficult for a free discussion of these issues to take place. Above all, the decentralized character of German political life meant that a coherent approach to population problems would run into trouble in coordinating the very different positions of German *Lander*, or states (McIntosh, 1983, ch. 6). It took the downturn in fertility in the 1960s to reopen the possibility of a new phase of political responses to population problems.

In Eastern Europe, the rise in the birth rate that followed the Second World War was in large part a compensatory reaction to the appalling human losses suffered among civilians and soldiers on the Eastern Front. No one will ever know the full toll of human life suffered by the people of those states that formed the Warsaw Pact in the postwar decade. The trend toward fertility decline in many countries of Eastern Europe had begun before 1939, but fertility levels in Eastern Europe were, on the whole, well above those of Western Europe. By the mid-1950s, the temporary surge of postwar births had largely ended, and the trend toward lower fertility was accelerated by new more liberal legislation on abortion introduced by the Soviet Union in 1955 and by other Eastern-bloc countries shortly thereafter.

Alarm about declining fertility therefore postdates the period under review in this chapter and is discussed in the following chapter. And although some tremulous voices were raised about the perils of low fertility, a source of complacency on this question in Eastern Europe may also have been ideological: the belief that the "victory" of socialism in the wake of the military successes of the Red Army in itself would lead citizens of the new socialist states to increase their fertility (Besemeres, 1980, passim).

Fertility and Population Growth, 1965-1984   5

THE DECLINE OF FERTILITY SINCE THE MID-1960s

Beginning in the mid-1960s, a new (yet old) phenomenon appeared in much of the Western world. Once more, the trend of fertility turned downward, reaching or even going beyond the low fertility levels of the 1930s. These declines were remarkably homogeneous in the otherwise socially diverse nations of the West; with few exceptions, there was a sharp "break" in period fertility rates around 1965. Declines between 1965 and about 1975 were sharp and nearly continuous, giving rise to a new sobriquet, the "baby bust." The decline began to level off after 1975, and in some countries there have been modest increases in period fertility since then.

So rapid were the fertility declines in the decade 1965–1975 that fertility rates often reached levels that would have been considered unbelievable in the mid-1960s. No demographer predicted such a dramatic or homogeneous decline (nor, for that matter, had any demographer anticipated the magnitude of the postwar baby boom in the United States). Fertility levels in most industrialized countries are now at levels below replacement, that is, the roughly 2.1 children per woman required for replacement of one generation of women by another given low mortality experience. As may be seen in Figures 4.1–4.7, such low levels of fertility were first recorded in Eastern Europe. The first Western European country to register below-replacement fertility was Sweden in 1968, followed in turn by Denmark and Finland in 1969; by Belgium, England and Wales, and the Netherlands in 1973; by France and Norway in 1975; by Italy in 1976; by Portugal in 1980; and by Spain in 1981. Fertility in the United States declined below replacement in 1972. Total fertility rates declined to a level as low as 1.38 in West Germany in 1978 and 1979, 1.43 in Denmark in 1982, and 1.50 in Switzerland in 1978 (Calot and Blayo, 1982, p. 351).

For the two largest countries of the industrialized world, the Soviet Union and the United States, fertility has been sustained at somewhat higher levels: 2.28 in the Soviet Union in 1979 and 1980 (see Appendix A), and about 1.8 in the United States. The higher level for the Soviet Union is attributable in part to the notably high levels of total fertility in the Central Asian republics: as late as 1979 and 1980, fertility levels of four to six children per woman were recorded, that is, levels comparable to those of India. Meanwhile, the fertility of the European Soviet republics was below replacement.

Given our interest in earlier fears of population decline, it is important to recognize that recent period fertility levels have often been substantially lower than those that stimulated so much concern during the 1930s. For example, the lowest period total fertility rate seen in the United States during the Great Depression was 2.19 children per woman, whereas levels somewhat below 1.85 have been sustained since 1974. In Germany in the 1930s, the lowest total fertility rate registered was 1.58 in 1933; in 1975 the West German rate was 1.45 and the East German rate was 1.54.

The sharp declines in fertility in the late 1960s and 1970s appear to be due to two factors that operated in the same direction: a decline in cohort fertility and a deferral of marriages and births. With regard to cohort fertility, we cannot be entirely sure about what ultimate fertility level will characterize the cohorts reaching reproductive age in the mid-1960s, as many of them have not yet completed their childbearing years. However, a clear pattern of decline in both fertility expectations and performance has arisen in these cohorts. For example, an American study showed that women aged 18–24 desired an average of 2.1 children in 1977, down fully 25% from the 2.8 children desired 6 years earlier (U.S. Bureau of the Census, 1977; U.S. House of Representatives, 1978, p. 18).

More concretely, during the 1960s there was available for the first time a set of acceptable, highly effective, and apparently medically safe methods of fertility control. These included the first contraceptive pills and the intrauterine device (IUD), both of which reached the market in substantial numbers in the mid-1960s. During the 1970s, doubts about the safety of both of these contraceptive methods were voiced, and this did lead to a modest reduction in the proportion of women using them. However, until the mid-1970s the contraceptive pill remained the single most popular form of fertility regulation in many Western countries.

The development of safe and acceptable forms of voluntary sterilization, especially the male vasectomy, also became widely practiced for the first time in the 1960s. This is a means of fertility truncation rather than regulation, and hence it is a method of choice primarily for couples who have achieved their desired family size. Nonetheless, sterilization became a very popular means of fertility control during the 1970s, to the extent that voluntary sterilization (both male and female) became the single most common form of fertility control in the United States in the mid-1970s, surpassing even the contraceptive pill (Ford, 1978, Table 1; Westoff and Jones, 1977, pp. 153–157).

A cautionary note is in order here. The temptations of a wholly technological explanation for the fertility decline seen since the 1960s must be tempered by the recognition that very low levels of fertility also had been recorded in the 1930s, when the only fertility regulation methods available were condoms, diaphragms, abstinence, and illegal abortion.

Finally, fertility levels were also affected by a nearly universal trend toward liberalization of abortion laws in Western countries, beginning in the 1960s and accelerating in the 1970s. By the end of that decade, abortion was substantially legal in virtually every country in Western Europe and North America, and in 1978 abortion was legalized even in Italy despite the strenuous opposition of the Vatican.

These trends of improved technology and of increased availability of fertility control contributed not only to a general decline in fertility across Western countries, but also to a reduction in fertility differentials among socioeconomic, racial, ethnic, and other social groups. For example, in the United States fertility has declined among both whites and blacks; although black fertility continues to exceed that of whites, longstanding differentials have been reduced over time. Similarly, the contraceptive behavior of American Roman Catholics was markedly transformed over this period, such that by 1975, with the exception of sterilization, it was no longer possible to distinguish between Catholic and non-Catholic birth control practices (Westoff and Jones, 1977, pp. 203–207).

A contrary trend to the fertility decline was the common experience of rising levels of teenage pregnancy and out-of-wedlock births in most Western countries. According to one estimate, fully 40% of all teenage girls in the United States became pregnant, and one-third of all teenage births were out of wedlock in the 1970s. With the decline in fertility among married women in their 20s and 30s over the same period, births to younger or unmarried women came to represent an increasing proportion of total births as compared to previous years. In the United States, out-of-wedlock births comprised over 14% of all births by the mid-1970s. In Denmark, there was a doubling of this percentage in the decade preceding 1974, reaching nearly 19% in that year. In Sweden, the comparable figure reached nearly one-third by the mid-1970s, nearly tripling from earlier figures (Westoff, 1978, p. 80).

Nonetheless, teenage fertility rates also *declined* somewhat over the same period, partly in concert with the overall fertility decline and partly because many teenage pregnancies were terminated under the liberalized abortion policy. In 1980, for example, teenage women accounted for nearly 30% of all legal abortions versus only 16% of all births (Henshaw and O'Reilly, 1983, p. 6; National Center for Health Statistics, 1982, p. 10).

Another important change in demographic behavior was the increase in the proportions never marrying and in the numbers of unmarried couples of opposite sex living together. In the United States, 43% of women aged 20–24 had not yet married in 1976, as compared to 28% in 1960. The comparable figures for Denmark were 59% in 1975 versus 44% in 1970. Meanwhile in Sweden the number of marriages declined by 30% between 1966 and 1975.

There have also been apparent increases in the numbers of cohabiting unmarried couples. In the United States the number of such relationships reached nearly 1 million by 1976, moving the U.S. Bureau of the Census to formulate a new statistical concept—POSSLQ—denoting persons of opposite sex sharing living quarters. In Denmark the number of cohabiting couples increased from 200,000 to 300,000 between 1974 and 1976, while in Sweden some 12% of all couples living together aged 16–70 were not married as of the early 1970s (Westoff, 1978, p. 80).

In important respects, the decline of fertility of the late 1960s onward represented a mirror image of the baby boom increases of the 1950s—substantial deferral of marriage, along with deferral of first births within marriage. Use of period fertility rates exaggerates the magnitude of the fertility decline as compared with cohort rates; this too is a mirror image of the baby boom, when period rates rose more than the underlying cohort rates. The early postwar phase was one of movement toward earlier childbearing, while the more recent period has been the reverse—a move toward later childbearing. Calot and Blayo (1982, pp. 361–362) presented in useful graphic form a comparison of the trends in period and cohort rates for six European countries: England and Wales, West Germany, France, Italy, the Netherlands, and Sweden (see Figure 5.1). In all but Italy, these data show a clear tendency for the period rates to exceed the cohort rates from about 1950 to 1970 and then the reverse pattern of cohort exceeding period rates since then.

Still, despite the exaggerated trendline provided by the period rates, between 1965 and 1984 real declines in cohort rates were clearly under way in all of the countries studied except Sweden. In many cases there appear to have been increases in the number of childless and one-child couples.

Easterlin argued that the baby bust can be explained by the same generational theory he employed to explain the preceding boom. The reproductive generations of the current period are themselves the offsprings of the baby boom, and hence in Easterlin's view have had the opposite experience of their parental generation: high cohort competition for available occupational slot and hence a pessimistic attitude leading to the deferred marriage and low fertility of the 1970s and 1980s. On this basis, another baby boom may occur in the 1990s, as the small birth cohorts of the baby bust reach reproductive age (Easterlin, 1980; for a popularization of his views, see Wolfe, 1977).

Still other demographers have adopted a variant of Becker's theory of opportunity costs of childbearing to account for the post-1965 fertility decline. Ermisch (1983) has argued that the gap between real wages for men and women narrowed after 1965, making it rational for women to choose work over childbearing. Here again mechanisms governing the "baby boom" are simply reversed to explain post-1965 developments.

Finally, there are those who do not dismiss Easterlin's hypoth-

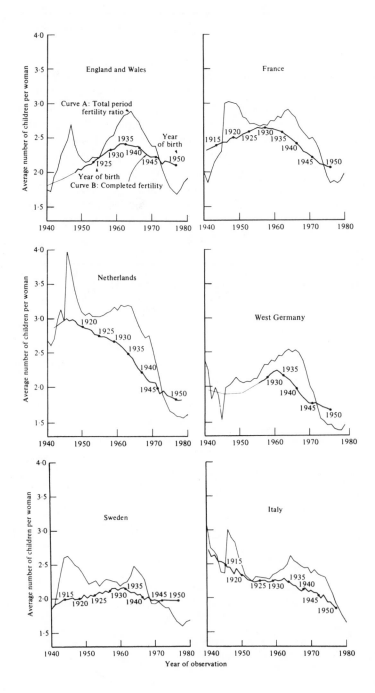

esis, but still believe that the postwar baby boom is an aberrational departure from a long-term fertility decline stretching over a century or more, and that it is this boom rather than the subsequent bust that requires explanation. The long-term fertility decline is attributed to changing social values, economic circumstances, and improved fertility control technologies. Westoff (1983), for example, argued that there are no

> social changes on the horizon that would lead to the expectation that the fertility rate will increase substantially (to a total fertility rate greater than 2.5, for example). More likely is the continuation of rates at or below replacement, and in some instances these rates may indeed fall closer to the one- than the two-child average. (p. 102)

CONTRASTING DEVELOPMENTS IN THE THIRD WORLD: THE "POPULATION EXPLOSION"

While the industrialized world of the 1945–1984 period recorded a varied and changing set of fertility patterns, ranging from sustained boom to short-term boomlet to sustained baby bust, the newly emerging nations of the third world entered a dramatic phase of natural demographic increase. This phenomenon was often described by the shorthand phrase "the population bomb"— a misleading title, since a bomb explodes with great force that is spent almost immediately. In contrast, the rapid growth of population is at glacial rates when compared to the expansive force of a bomb but generates a long-lasting momentum that sustains growth for 50 to 70 years. Whether bomb or glacier, the dramatic growth of postwar population was stimulated by the rapid declines in mortality that had begun in many developing countries before the Second World War and continued at least until the 1970s. Mortality declines were especially dramatic for infants and children, with infant mortality rates sometimes declining by as much as 40

Figure 5.1 Comparison of the total period fertility ratio and completed fertility for the period 1940–1980 for England and Wales, France, the Netherlands, West Germany, Sweden, and Italy. The heavier curve, which has the year of the mothers' birth indicated, is the completed fertility curve. The lighter curve is the total period fertility ratio, or the period total fertility rate. (Source: Calot and Blayo, 1982.)

percent in only 15 years, as was the case in Venezuela between 1945 and 1959.

There is considerable debate as to the sources of these dramatic mortality declines. Some attribute them to the rapid spread of cheap and effective public health and sanitation technologies developed in the industrialized world. Others hold that the improvement of food production and transportation reduced the toll of localized famines. Finally, some believe that the improvement of administrative capacities of governments in these areas enabled them to determine needs for emergency food and medicine and to meet them in a way that earlier, less-effective governments had found impossible (Preston, 1978; for a contrary view, see Sen, 1981; for infant mortality decline, see U.N. Statistical Office, 1968, Table 14).

Whatever the reasons, the demographic effects can scarcely be doubted. The rate of natural increase in the third world as a whole accelerated by nearly two-thirds, from about 1.44% in the decade 1940–1950 to 2.38% in 1970 (U.N. Statistical Office, 1964, Table 2). Countries in Latin America such as El Salvador experienced annual population growth rates in excess of 3.5% in the period 1965–1970, which, if sustained, would double the population in less than 20 years. In at least one case, that of Kenya, population growth was estimated at 4% per year around 1980, implying a doubling time of only 17 years.

Rates of such magnitude gave rise to their own form of alarmism, with publication in the 1960s of books bearing titles such as *The Population Bomb* (Ehrlich, 1968) and *Famine, 1975!* (Paddock and Paddock, 1968). More restrained attention was given the subject within international aid agencies (led especially by Sweden) concerned with the economic development of third world countries, and eventually within the United Nations system (Piotrow, 1973, ch. 19; Warwick, 1982).

The rapid population growth rates of the third world peaked during the 1970s, and by the end of the decade had been reduced slightly, principally due to fertility declines in a few large developing countries such as the People's Republic of China (which alone accounts for over one-quarter of the third world population), Indonesia, Mexico, Brazil, and Colombia. The pace of fertility decline in these countries was substantial, but in other major countries such as India, Pakistan, Bangladesh, Nigeria, and Egypt there were only modest (if any) fertility reductions. Meanwhile, mortality declines continued apace. Hence the crude annual rate of population growth in the third world taken together declined only modestly, from about 2.4% in the period 1970–1975 to 2.1% in the period 1975–1980.

During the same period, the fertility declines in the industrialized world led to crude annual rates of natural increase almost universally less than 0.5%, and in some cases to small negative rates (e.g., −0.15% in West Germany in 1980 and −0.06% in Denmark in 1981 (Council of Europe, 1982, Table 1b).

Somewhat surprisingly, relatively little attention has been paid so far, by both analysts and alarmists alike, to the sharp differentials in demographic growth rates that resulted from the convergence of low growth in the industrialized world and very rapid growth in the third world. Occasional references are made to the notable fact that by the year 2000 nearly 80% of the world's population will be in the third world (U.N. Population Division, 1981, p. 6), but generally this has not raised the specter of the Yellow Peril and similar nightmares that had haunted discussions earlier in the century (but see the remarks of one French politician in Chapter 6, p. 124). This may reflect a realization that military security no longer depends upon the number of bodies available to man the trenches, but more upon the level of technology so central to the nuclear age.

A possibly significant expression of older concerns did arise in 1984, at the initiative of the government of France. At an informal meeting in Paris in April, the ministers of the Ministries of Social Affairs and Employment of the 10 nations of the European Economic Community (EEC) were asked to support a French proposal for an EEC initiative to deal with the demographic situation in Europe, which the proposal described as a cause for serious anxiety. Reportedly, only the minister from Luxembourg supported the French position (*Population and Development Review*, 1984a, p. 569). But a week later the European Parliament adopted a "Resolution on the need for community measures to promote population growth in Europe (No. C127/78, 14 May 1984). This resolution notes "the disappointing outcome of the informal meeting of the Ministers for Social Affairs and Employment in Paris on 5 April 1984" and calls for "measures to combat this marked trend toward population decline." In a clear echo of French opinion before the First World War, it points to the declining percentage of the world's population accounted for by Europe and links this and population "vitality" to "Europe's standing and influence in the world." The full text in translation of this resolution is reproduced as Appendix B.

TRENDS IN INTERNATIONAL MIGRATION

One of the most important demographic changes of the 1960s and 1970s was not perceived as such at the time. During this period there was a rapid acceleration of international migration from the third world to the West.

In the case of Western Europe, much of what proved to be permanent immigration was not intended to be such, but was seen rather as temporary worker or "guest-worker" migration, in which needed labor would be imported for short periods to fill bottlenecks in the booming Western European economies. The intention was that all of the temporary migrants would return home after a year or two, along with their savings and newly learned skills that would be of use to the economic development of their home countries.

In practice, however, there were strong economic incentives for employers to renew contracts with temporary workers, so as to keep wages from rising and to avoid the need for perennial training programs. Meanwhile, religious and political activists began to assert the rights of these migrants to remain in Western Europe if they so wished. Combined with economic instability in much of the third world, such pressures led to the retention of some 5 million of the 30 million migrant workers. These 5 million have now become an unexpected permanent part of the Western European labor force and have been joined by more than 8 million people in their immediate and extended families. Hence over the past two decades approximately 13 million third world residents have in this way immigrated permanently to Western Europe; in addition to these 13 million, there are those admitted with the intention of permanent residence in the first place (Miller and Martin, 1982, Table 2.5).

Another unexpected consequence of these short-term labor importation programs was that they proved easier to start than to stop. The European programs and earlier ones in the United States resulted in well-established immigration "pathways" through which migrants continued to move even after the initial labor-importation policies were halted. In part, continuing immigration involved family members of previously admitted temporary workers who had been able to establish permanent residence for the economic and political reasons just discussed. In addition to this, the temporary worker programs made it widely known in the sending countries that there were high wages and ready employment in the receiving countries, making immigration an attractive option for increasing numbers of people. Hence, when the legal labor-importation policies were ended, migration continued clandestinely, giving rise to the now-serious problems of illegal immigration (Martin and Sehgal, 1980, pp. 207–229; U.N. Population Division, 1982, ch. 4).

In the United States in the 1960s and particularly in the 1970s, there occurred rapid growth in both legal and illegal immigration. Legal immigration increased primarily due to important reforms in U.S. immigration law that were passed in 1965 and that took full effect in 1968. In addition, there were large numbers of refugees admitted during this period from Cuba, Eastern Europe, and Indochina.

The growth of illegal immigration to the United States during the 1970s is tied to the temporary worker (bracero) program of the period 1942–1964. But throughout the last three decades, the level of illegal immigration cannot be measured with any confidence since those involved do not wish to be enumerated by an official agency. However, it was estimated that by 1978 there were between 3.5 and 6 million illegal aliens resident in the United States, most of whom had entered during the 1970s (Siegel, Passell, and Robinson, 1981, appen. E, pp. 13–29).

The convergence of the baby bust with the growth of international migration has led to a new demographic phenomenon of great relevance to debates about population decline. Put simply, the combination of record-low fertility and high immigration (especially from countries of higher fertility than the receiving countries) means that immigration must account for a large and increasing proportion of Western population growth. In countries such as West Germany, where natural increase is now slightly negative, *all* of the demographic increase is accounted for by immigration. Moreover, a substantial fraction of births in West Germany are produced by Turkish and other immigrants. In the United States, which has a younger age distribution and higher fertility than West Germany, the high level of immigration and the baby bust mean that more than one-third of total demographic increase is attributable to immigration; again, reliable estimation is impossible here, given the lack of credible statistics on the magnitude of illegal immigration. We shall return to the subject of immigration in the section entitled "Demographic and Economic Significance of Immigration" in Chapter 6.

POLITICAL AND IDEOLOGICAL MOVEMENTS

The increasing availability of effective means of fertility regulation in the 1960s was related to increased public support for provision of birth control advice and devices in almost all Western countries. Whereas in the 1950s American President Dwight Eisenhower said "I cannot imagine anything more emphatically a subject that is not a proper political or governmental activity or function or responsibility than questions of reproduction" (Piotrow, 1973, p. 45), by 1970 the American Congress was able to pass legislation that provided free fertility regulation services to all persons unable to obtain them in the private health sector. Opposition among physicians to contraception and other means of fertility regulation declined over the same period, and by the 1970s there was either benign or active support for such services in the medical profession.

Over the same period there arose political activist movements concerned with environmental preservation, freedom of choice about abortion, and feminism, and all of these tended to advocate either fertility declines or the rights of women to have access to fertility control methods.

Partly in response, there arose in the 1970s the pro-life or right-to-life movements, which focused initially upon prohibiting voluntary abortion. Later some pro-life groups expanded their focus to include opposition to contraceptives such as the IUD and the pill and to government-supported family planning programs (Vinovskis, 1980, pp. 224–261).

The Environmental Movement

The environmental movement was in many ways a creature of the baby boom, stimulated in part by alarms about the population explosion. Its intellectual roots may be traced to the antinuclear movement in Japan and to the growth of concern about urban and rural pollution in the United States in the 1960s, a concern often expressed by the baby boom generation. By the late 1970s the movement had taken on a new and more politicized form in Western Europe, with the Greens entering the Bundestag on a platform that was at once antinuclear, environmentalist, and politically radical. (For a literary perspective on the German debate, see Grass, 1982).

Some important American environmentalists were also population alarmists, and support for environmentalism was stimulated by Ehrlich's 1968 book *The Population Bomb*. There arose in the early 1970s an array of environmentalist lobby groups, from the Environmental Defense Fund to Zero Population Growth Inc. The latter organization, whose honorary chairman is Paul Ehrlich, often expresses its concern about population growth in terms of its negative effects upon the environment (*ZPG Reports*, 1983).

The Abortion Reform and Feminist Movements

Other political currents helped reinforce the trend toward declining fertility in the post-1965 period. The first is the generalized movement toward more liberal abortion laws that began in Eastern Europe in the 1950s and in Western Europe in the 1960s. In the case of Eastern Europe, the origins of these reforms were largely attributable to the new political dominance of the Soviet Union, given the traditional Leninist argument that abortion was a basic right of the woman to control her own body. As noted in Chapter 2, however, such basic rights were sharply limited during the 1930s in the Soviet Union, when concern rose about low fertility. However, recently, Soviet and other Marxists have not always viewed contraception in a similar light, but instead have seen it at times as a retrograde and Malthusian measure aimed solely at population checks unnecessary under socialism (DiMaio, 1981, pp. 157-178; Keyfitz, 1972, pp. 56-59).

In Western Europe and North America, abortion reform was placed on the political agenda by liberal and left groups opposed in principle to statutory limits on the rights of women to control their own fertility, and by physicians and others concerned with preventive health care and family planning. In the United States, agitation for reform was directed toward constitutional challenges to state laws restricting access to abortion. In Western Europe, the road to reform was via legislation. (U.N. Fund for Population Activities, 1979).

From the late 1960s, the case for abortion was embraced by the feminist movement, which had reappeared in a revitalized form. Feminism is a house of many mansions, but in the mainstream commitment to the right to abortion is a sine qua non of feminism. Meanwhile, contraception raises questions to which feminists have given a variety of answers.

Most feminists saw (and continue to see) abortion in terms of the fundamental right of a woman to control her own body, much as Lenin believed. However, most feminists also rejected the view, loosely attributed to Marx, that contraception was Malthusian and therefore objectionable (Boston Women's Health Book Collective, 1976).

The feminist viewpoint is an attitude toward reproductive rights, and not primarily about any one means of fertility limitation. As such, its goal is liberating women from being told what to do or not to do by (usually male) members of the medical profession or others, and allowing women to make up their own minds about methods of contraception on the basis of informed choice. Within this context, feminists have objected to medical control over access to most contraceptive devices as well as to what they consider the cavalier attitude of some doctors to the health risks attached to certain contraceptive methods such as oral contraceptives and intrauterine devices (IUDs). (Boston Women's Health Book Collective, 1976; Seamen, 1969).

The medical questions raised by feminists deserve careful attention, and surely there continues to be some division of medical opinion about the health risks of oral contraceptives.The majority view among medical specialists is that they are safe and effective for most women (exceptions include women over 35 years old, especially those who smoke). Some studies report further that the pill appears, if anything, to reduce the incidence of breast and uterine cancer—the opposite of earlier concerns about possible carcinogenicity—and thereby has contributed to decreasing reproductive mortality to unprecedently low levels (R. D. Gambrell, Jr., R. C. Maier, and B. I. Sanders, 1983; S. Ramcharan, F. A. Pellegrin, R. Ray, and J-P. Hsu, 1981). Other studies have suggested, however, that the cancer risks of oral contraceptives may be real after all (M. P. Vessey, K. McPherson, M. Lawless, and D. Yeates, 1983; M. C. Pike, M. D. Krailo, B. E. Henderson, A. Duke, and S. Roy, 1983). It is clear that both the medical and feminist debates on this matter are far from over.

The Pro-Life or Right-to-Life Movements

In the 1970s there was a political reaction to the prior liberalization of contraceptive and abortion laws in Western countries. A variety of groups (describing themselves initially as right-to-life and later as pro-life advocates) coalesced initially in opposition to the trend toward legalized abortion that accelerated in the late 1960s. Many of these groups received strong support from churches and other religious groups, and some formed grass-roots political organizations or, in a few cases, full-fledged political parties. (In New York State there is a statewide Right to Life party, which runs a slate of candidates from governor on down.) In some cases, the groups' opposition to legalized abortion was extended to include contraceptives that might impede implantation of fertilized ova (such as the IUD and oral contraceptives), which were deemed therefore effectively to be abortifacients.

It is fair to say that the pro-life movement has been successful on the political level in some Western countries and most notably in the United States. Pro-life proponents have succeeded in prohibiting government-financed domestic health and international assistance programs from providing abortion services, and government research programs from financing research on abortion techniques. There has been a concerted attack on Planned Parenthood and other service providers, with pro-life fringe elements spinning off in the direction of condoning or being responsible for terrorist bombings.

The non-violent part of the pro-life movement has the declared support of President Reagan and of a number of important members of Congress. In 1981 the leader of one pro-life group, Marjorie Mecklenberg, was appointed deputy assistant secretary in the Department of Health and Human Services with responsibility for many federal family planning programs; and Dr. C. Everett Koop, a candidate supported by pro-life groups, became the U.S. surgeon general. In 1984, a long-time pro-life politician, former Senator James Buckley, was appointed head of the U.S. delegation to the United Nations International Conference on Population in Mexico City. Senator Buckley insisted upon a review of well-established U.S. policy on population, which resulted in a new policy statement presented at the Mexico City conference. This document, reproduced in full as Appendix C, shows signs of hasty compromise between opposing forces within the Reagan administration. It restates long-standing American refusal to finance abortion services in developing countries, adding that nations that do support abortion services with non-U.S. funds will be required to set up segregated accounting procedures. It also, for the first time, declares that the United States will not "contribute to separate nongovernmental organizations which perform or actively promote abortion as a method of family planning in other nations." It is unclear how this declaration will be implemented in practice.

For our purposes though, the most interesting part of the new political position of the Reagan administration is not its attacks on abortion, but the attempt in its new policy statement to reconceptualize the role of demographic change in relation to economic growth. While past U.S. statements have described rapid population growth as an impediment to economic growth in developing countries, the new statement describes such rapid growth as "of itself, a neutral phenomenon." It states further that in the past there has been an "overreaction" to rapid population growth, which it attributes to "an outbreak of anti-intellectualism" in the West and the growth of " 'economic statism.' " It acknowledges no general problem of excessive demographic increase in the third world, but rather only "localized crises," which it sees as evidence of "too much government control and planning, rather than too little." In short, the best way to deal with so-called problems of population is the adoption of a "non-statist" economic system based on free markets.

This section of the policy statement marshalls arguments similar to those of an enthusiastic proponent of continued population growth, Julian L. Simon. In a remarkably forthright introduction to one of his more popular works, Simon candidly admitted that he experienced a conversion from strong Malthusian views to his current pronatalism and that this dramatic shift was tied to a period of emotional upheaval in his life (Simon, 1981, p. 9). This, of course, is reminiscent of many of the statements of early exponents of the fear of population decline, whose policy and personal concerns were also inextricably intertwined (e.g., Zola; see p. 25).

Since his volte-face, Simon has been arguing with the enthusiasm of a convert that the long-term effects of population growth are positive—that it stimulates economic growth, technological advance, cultural creativity, and the like. ("Have I gone crazy," he reported musing at the time of his conversion, "What business do I have trying to help arrange it that fewer human beings will be born, each one of whom might be a Mozart or a Michelangelo or an Einstein. . . . ?") (1981, pp. 9–10). Although both his analyses and recommendations have been criticized strongly by most other scholars of the subject, they have fallen on fertile ground among pro-life activists seeking intellectual justification for the extension of their opposition from abortion to contraception.

During the year before the preparation of the policy statement, Simon moved to Washington and became a senior fellow of the Heritage Foundation, a conservative institute with close ties to ideological elements within the Reagan administration. Thus Simon's arguments in favor of continued population growth, though they have much in common with those of the Communist leadership of Rumania and other Eastern European countries (see discussion later in this chapter), also proved attractive to conservative U.S. intellectuals, who apparently were unaware of the parallels with Communist thought on this matter. We cannot be sure that the policy statement's radical departure from long-standing U.S. government interpretations of population issues had anything to do with the Heritage Foundation and its pronatalist senior fellow. But the episode does illustrate once again the attractiveness of pronatalist ideas to ideologists of both the right and the left.

The final three sections of the 1984 U.S. policy statement appear to have been hastily inserted after the initial draft was circulated in Washington and are notably lacking in harmony with the arguments in the first two sections. They affirm that the United States will continue to help developing countries "slow their population growth through support for effective voluntary family planning programs." This policy is based on the economic argument that rapid population growth "compounds already serious problems" of development, and that such assistance improves "the quality of life of mothers and children."

Thus the policy statement represents an uneasy, even self-contradictory, amalgam of divergent views. Opposition to abortion is forcefully stated, in concert with the strongly held views of pro-life groups and of the head of the delegation; population problems, if such exist, are attributed to "economic statism," in concert with the views of the libertarian fringe of the Republican administration; but there is also a reaffirmation of economic arguments for continued assistance for family planning programs, which have had strong support among the public and the Congress for the past decade. How the balance between these divergent positions will shift in the future is, of course, an open question.

TRENDS IN EASTERN EUROPE AND THE SOVIET UNION

Eastern European demographic experience has been strikingly different from that in Western Europe, as described in the previous two chapters. Much of Eastern Europe did not experience below-replacement fertility during the 1930s (see Tables 4.6–4.7), and fertility at the end of the Second World War was higher than in Western Europe. But the postwar fertility declines began earlier in Eastern Europe, reached below-replacement levels earlier (i.e., in the 1960s), and then rose either modestly or dramatically in response to a generalized pronatalist policy adopted throughout the region. At the risk of some oversimplification, it is sensible to discuss the Eastern European experience in three parts: that of the Soviet Union, of Rumania, and of the rest of the Eastern European countries.

The Soviet Union

Soviet fertility levels declined only modestly from the late 1950s to the late 1970s, that is, from a total fertility rate of 2.8 in 1958–1959 to 2.3 in 1979–1980. The most dramatic aspect of Soviet demography over the period was the very large differential in fertility between the Slavic and Baltic republics as compared to those of the Transcaucasian and Central Asian republics. The Slavic and Baltic republics in 1979 and 1980 recorded relatively uniform fertility levels near or below replacement, ranging from 1.9 in the Russian Republic and Latvia to 2.4 in Moldavia. In the Transcaucasian region the range was considerably higher, from 2.2 to 3.3. And in the Central Asian republics, fertility as recently as in 1979 and 1980 was extraordinarily high for an industrialized country, ranging from 4.1 in Kirgizia to 5.8 in Tadzhikistan (Feshbach, 1982, Table 5).

While the latter two categories represent distinctly minority populations of the Soviet Union, the long-term demographic implications of such large differentials in fertility were not lost upon Soviet policymakers. The Russian population of the Soviet Union, while still representing 52.4% of the total population in 1979, was projected to decline to 46.7% by the year 2000. Meanwhile, the population of Muslims (mostly in the Central Asian republics) was projected to increase from 16.7% in 1979 to 21.3% in the year 2000. As Feshbach (1982) has noted:

> The implications of this disparity for future labor supplies and military manpower must be of major concern for the Russians in the Kremlin. With the national fertility decline of the past decade and a half, annual additions to the population of working age will drop sharply during the 1980s and virtually all net increases will come from high-fertility, non-Slavic regions. By 2000, one-third of all 18-year-old males available for the required two years of military service will come from the southern republics, compared to 18 percent in 1970, while the share of 18-year-old males in the Russian republic drops from 56 percent to 44 percent. (p. 5)

One of the most puzzling aspects of recent demographic trends in the Soviet Union is the apparent increase in death rates for infants, and for males from age 20-44, in particular. Some of the increase may be due to improving registration of death, but a real mortality increase does seem to have occurred. The reasons for this are not clear; one explanation is that medical facilities may be too few or too unevenly distributed and utilized for the needs of the population, compounded by further problems of shortages in medical equipment and medicines and rampant alcoholism, especially among Slavic males (Davis and Feshbach, 1980; *New York Times*, 21 June 1981).

Whatever the reasons for these differentials and trends, at the 26th Communist Party Congress of February 1981, a new set of measures apparently aimed at encouraging fertility was announced, with the stated goals of improving life for "families with children, newlyweds, the growing generation, and above all, women" (Feshbach, 1982, p. 3). These measures, which are to cost 9 billion rubles (U.S. $12.2 billion) over a 5-year period, include lump-sum grants of 50 rubles for first births and 100 rubles for second and third births. These replace previous birth grant payments that began only with the third birth and were much smaller in magnitude.

Child allowances for unmarried mothers rose, but for others, they were generally not increased under the new program. Partially paid maternity leave is to be granted to working mothers for a year after birth, replacing the previous system of unpaid maternity leave. Other measures that appeared to be aimed at stimulating fertility were authorized, including more part-time employment opportunities for mothers, the barring of women from 460 occupations involving heavy or hazardous work, more and better day-care facilities for preschool children, improved housing conditions, additional leave days for mothers of two or more children under 12, and measures to assist in housework for working mothers (Feshbach, 1982, p. 4).

Rumania

Rumania represents an extreme case of the generalized pronatalism that has characterized the Socialist states of Eastern Europe since the mid-1960s. Abortion was legalized in Rumania in 1957.

Abortions were readily available, the fee was low (less than U.S. $2 in 1957), and the medical danger slight. Consistent with the practice of other Marxist–Leninist governments, contraception was not encouraged, and as a result by 1966 there was near-total dependence upon abortion for fertility control. Abortion rates rose rapidly and fertility declined sharply, with the period total fertility rate declining from 3.07 in 1955 to 1.80 in 1966—a decline of over 40% in just over a decade.

The Rumanian government's response to this fertility decline can only be described as draconian. In a setting in which abortion had been allowed to serve as virtually the sole means of fertility regulation, abortion was essentially banned without warning in November 1966. At the same time, a full array of pronatalist measures were adopted, including restrictions on access to modern contraceptives and to divorce, and increases in birth premiums, tax benefits, housing preferences, maternity leaves, and retirement benefits for parents, especially for those with two or more children.

The results were dramatic indeed, no doubt exceeding the expectations of those formulating the pronatalist policy. Total fertility in 1967 was 3.66, over 100% higher than that in 1966. A large proportion of the increased births were concentrated during only a few months of 1967, resulting in serious overcrowding of maternity facilities. At the same time a shortage of obstetrical expertise arose because many Rumanian physicians were female and were on maternity leave. These and other factors led to sharp increases in both infant and maternal mortality.

Subsequentally, Rumanian fertility declined by over one-third from its peaks in 1967 and 1968, with the total fertility rate reaching 2.43 by 1980. Although a comparable measure of fertility is not available for more recent years, trends in the crude birth rate suggest that fertility has continued to decline at least through 1983 (see p. 102).

The effects upon the Rumanian age structure of such an accordion-like expansion and contraction of fertility are equally dramatic. The cohorts born in the late 1960s were about twice as large as those born in the early 1960s. What effect such rapid changes in cohort size have had upon the quality of education and upon employment opportunities as these cohorts have grown older is unclear. Certainly the draconian Rumanian pronatalist policy of the late 1960s may be said to have had a significant demographic effect (Teitelbaum, 1972, pp. 419–439).

As mentioned, it appears that the Rumanian birth rate continued to decline through 1983, when it again reached the pre-1967 level. This decline led the central committee of the Rumanian Communist party to issue a forceful reassertion of its pronatalist policy. In a March 1984 resolution, the party's central committee noted the "intolerable situation" in which the birth rate had declined from 19.7 to 14.3 births per 1000 women between 1975 and 1983, and in which the number of abortions exceeded the number of live births by over 30%. It affirmed that "an increase in the birth rate, efforts to ensure adequate population growth, and the strengthening of the family must constitute priority objectives for the development of our socialist nation in order to ensure the economic and social progress of the country and preserve the vigor and youth of the entire people." (See Appendix D, in which the Rumanian central committee's resolution is reproduced in full, for this and subsequent quotations.)

To this end, the Rumanian Communist party formulated a set of measures to restrict access to abortion and to promote public information campaigns leading to a broader understanding that "the task of ensuring normal demographic growth in the population is a high honor and a patriotic duty . . . to ensure for our country successive new generations that will contribute to the prosperity of our socialist nation and to the triumph of socialism and communism in Rumania."

It is interesting to note that these measures were advanced at a time when the Rumanian population was growing, not declining in size. Moreover, the explicit goal is to "increase the birth rate to 19–20 per thousand population per year," implying a population growth rate approaching 1% over the indefinite future. The clear implication is that such a growth rate is what the Rumanian government takes to be "normal demographic growth."

Other Eastern European Countries

With the exceptions of Albania and East Germany, all Eastern European countries followed the Soviet lead in liberalizing abortion in the 1950s. Generalized fertility declines followed, which were typically received "with surprise, often with incredulity, and always with disapproval" (as cited in David and McIntyre, 1981, p. 77). In Czechoslovakia, concern was evident as early as 1957. Here, as well as in Hungary and Bulgaria, there quickly emerged a governmental view about the negative consequences of declining population growth, and measures were undertaken both to restrict access to abortion and to provide incentives for childbearing. Unlike parallel policies in the West, these Eastern European policies were adopted with the explicit aim of increasing fertility levels.

Restrictions upon abortion were far more moderate in the rest of Eastern Europe than in Rumania. Exceptions were allowed in special cases, but young women with fewer than two living children had some difficulty in obtaining abortions legally. At the same time, most of these countries adopted much greater economic inducements favoring fertility, including lengthy paid maternity leave, preferential housing and loan programs for large families, tax incentives, and progressive birth payments and substantial family allowances (see Chapter 7).

Overall such payments were high relative to prevailing incomes and strongly encouraged second- and third-order births. For example, in 1980 and 1981 a family with three children received family allowances amounting to 53% of the average manufacturing wage in Czechoslovakia (vs. 18% for a two-child family); 34% in Bulgaria (12% for two-child families); and 33% in Hungary (21% for two-child families). In Poland, where fertility levels have generally been considerably higher than in the rest of Eastern Europe, and in East Germany, the comparable payments were far less generous, and also less progressive (Frejka, 1982, Table 2).

As can be seen from a glance at Appendix A, most of these countries' recent fertility levels are in excess of replacement and are considerably higher than those in most Western nations. David and McIntyre (1981) stated that payments of such magnitude may reasonably be expected to have had a "definite, but not necessarily large, positive fertility response," but they considered it "too early to offer a general empirical conclusion." They noted further that whatever success has been achieved has incurred "very high budgetary cost" (pp. 86–87). But such issues form part of a discussion of the wider nature of population policy since 1965, which is the subject of the next chapter.

Policy Implications and Responses, 1965–1984   6

INTRODUCTION

In this chapter we examine the political and policy implications of the sharp fertility declines registered by many industrialized countries in the period 1965–1984, as a prelude to our discussion of future trends and options in Chapter 7. We first consider general policy questions, and then turn to the subject of specific initiatives in the United States, Western Europe, and the Soviet bloc. We conclude with a closer look at currents of opinion in France and Germany, where political debate on this subject retains much of the rhetoric we highlighted in Chapters 2 and 3.

GENERAL POLICY IMPLICATIONS

Since 1965, most discussions of the policy implications of fertility decline have centered on three facets of this demographic development: (1) the effects of changing age structures, (2) the slowing of aggregate population growth rates, and (3) the changing composition of national populations when low fertility is matched by substantial immigration.

Age Structure and Public Policy

Probably the most important of these facets are the shifts toward older age structures that resulted from the baby bust, changes that loom even larger in those Western countries that had earlier experienced sustained and substantial baby booms. It is no exaggeration to say that changes in a society's age structure are of significance for virtually all aspects of public policy. For purposes of concise discussion, we consider the effects of age structure in four main categories: (1) economic effects; (2) allocation and real-location between young and old; (3) societal character, including vigor, creativity, and the like; and (4) military manpower. In all cases, the discussion that follows necessarily takes the form of ceteris paribus, since it is obvious that all the aspects discussed are affected also by factors other than aging. Finally, while this chapter is intended as a survey of trends over the years 1965-1984, it is clear that the issues discussed here will be relevant to future discussions as well. For this reason, we shall extend these arguments in Chapter 7.

Economic Effects

The main economic effects of the aging of a population have to do with changes in the growth rate and composition of the labor force, and in the characteristics of the population as consumers and savers.

The likely effects of a labor force that is shifting gradually toward a higher proportion of older workers are numerous and complex. First, an aging labor force should have lower unemployment and higher productivity since unemployment and low productivity tend to be concentrated among young workers. In many industrialized countries such a tendency must be welcome after a decade of relatively high unemployment and low rates of productivity increase (which in some cases can be attributed partly, but only partly, to the rapid growth of the age groups born during the baby boom).

On the other hand, an older labor force could be more resistant to change than a younger one. An older worker might be less likely to undergo the educational or apprenticeship process again and conceivably be more set in his or her ways. An older labor force might also be more resistant to physical relocation in response to changing economic conditions since younger people with fewer family responsibilities are more likely to be mobile. If such resistance to change should appear, they would be of particular concern during a period of rapid technological innovation, requiring new skills and work practices and a willingness to relocate in areas where labor demand is high.

Obvious policy implications emerge from the above: the importance of improving mid-career education and retraining to help an aging labor force adapt to a changing economy, and the importance of public policies (e.g., regarding housing and relocation) to encourage a willingness to move as economic change occurs.

A related likely effect of an aging work force is the improvement (relative to older cohorts) of the economic and career fortunes of young workers over the coming several decades. In general, the small size of the age groups entering the work force is likely to increase their economic value to employers, especially when compared to circumstances of surplus labor that have prevailed recently as the baby boom has matured. Under these conditions, average wages to young workers should increase relative to those of older workers. In addition, there are likely to be better prospects for career advancement for these labor-force entrants, since there are relatively few of them compared with the older generations higher in the organizational hierarchy. Such improvements should be especially great among the categories of young workers that have been most marginal in recent years. The desperately high levels of minority youth unemployment in many industrialized countries can be expected to decline as employers find it to their economic advantage to recruit, train, and retain scarce workers. However, as suggested by Wachter (1979), such improvements could be short-circuited by large-scale importation of immigrant labor competing for similar entry-level jobs.

A gradual aging of the population seems likely to generate a slow change in the levels of aggregate and sectoral demand. On the one hand, declining numbers of young adults may lead to reduced demand for small housing units; fewer teenagers would imply smaller markets for teenage consumer goods such as popular music and clothing; and fewer children may reduce demand for child-oriented toys, clothing, and services. On the other hand, increasing proportions of middle-aged and older adults are likely to increase demand for family housing, family cars, adult education, and health care for these age groups.

In addition to such changes in the composition of demand, the "automatic" increase in the size of some markets due to increasing numbers of consumers will become less important, while at the same time per capita disposable income may increase, thereby possibly raising the marginal propensity to consume. It is difficult to anticipate the net effects of such offsetting trends, except to note that the declining significance of automatic market growth will increase the importance of high-quality management and planning by business and government.

With regard to savings and investment, if past patterns continue, an aging population can be expected to save and invest more than a younger population, thereby increasing the pool of capital available for productive investment. Such effects, however, are likely to be swamped by macroeconomic policies that favor or discourage savings, as demonstrated by the very high savings rates of the relatively youthful Japanese population over the past decade. (For Japanese national income statistics, see U.N. Statistical Office, 1980, vol. 1, pt. 1, pp. 726ff.)

Allocation and Reallocation between Young and Old

It seems fairly obvious that in a democratic nation, an aging population will gradually result in a relative reallocation of public resources away from the smaller cohorts of the young and toward the larger cohorts of the middle-aged and elderly. Such a reallocation in reverse occurred in some baby boom countries during the late 1950s and 1960s, with sharp (if belated) increases in public investment for primary and secondary education. More recently, there has been a gradual (and in some senses unintentional) reallocation toward the elderly retired population, resulting largely from the unexpected consequences of inflation indexing in public pensions and other age-related benefits, which were intended to protect the elderly from the ravages of inflationary fiscal and monetary policies adopted for other reasons (see Preston, 1984, pp. 44–49).

It is important to note that the posited reallocation from the youthful to the older cohorts concerns aggregate resources and does not preclude substantial per-capita increases for the younger groups. A strong case can be made for increasing per-capita investment in education and child health services, for example, given the greater societal "value" of the young deriving simply from their relative scarcity. In addition, those with an interest in maintaining high levels of aggregate resource allocation (e.g., education ministries and unions, and providers of other youth-oriented services) can be expected to argue, and to use their political power, to oppose cuts in such allocations.

One of the most hotly debated issues arising from an aging population is that of the future financial viability of pension or social security systems. Similar concerns have arisen about the long-term financing of health care. These contentious debates are discussed later in this chapter and in Chapter 7.

Societal Character

It is difficult to know how to assess assertions that older populations differ in character from younger ones. The French demographer Alfred Sauvy vividly characterized his image of an aging society as one comprised of "old people, living in old houses, ruminating about old ideas," (Teitelbaum, 1978, pp. xx–xxi). In this view, of course, Sauvy is in sympathy with much of the French pronatalist intellectual and political tradition discussed in Chapter 2. Are older societies more staid and conservative, less vigorous and creative, less productive economically, generally more boring, as commentators in the tradition of Sauvy would have it (Weber, 1977; Simon, 1981)?

Unfortunately, there is no empirical way to judge such pronouncements. Societies with the "oldest" populations include those of Sweden, West Germany, and the United Kingdom. It is at least doubtful whether the above characterizations apply accurately to them. Indeed many commentators would point to the large differences, rather than the similarities, in the economic productivity, political tenor, and cultural attributes of these three countries. Moreover, there would be strong disagreements as to whether the economic dynamism of West Germany is normatively "better" than the social stability and continuity of the United Kingdom.

Leaving aside such contentions, it is appropriate to mention one demographic reality. It is now well established that a low-fertility population *must*, as a mathematical certainty, be older than a high-fertility population (excluding the effects in either direction of migration). As long as mortality levels remain low (or decline further) in industrial countries, the kinds of fertility increases necessary to bring about significantly younger age structures imply substantial and continuing population growth (Coale, 1957, pp. 83–89). In short, it would be impossible, short of mortality increases or large-scale out-migration to have a population that is both more youthful and nongrowing. But here again, the question as to whether a continuing growth of population is desirable is largely a subjective choice.

Military Manpower

There has been some concern expressed over the last few years as to the future adequacy of available pools of military manpower should low fertility continue. In a sense such arguments represent muted echoes of earlier debates, especially in France, about the relationship of population growth to national military prowess (see Chapter 2). As recently as 1981, Sauvy attributed the nineteenth-century decline of French naval power to population aging caused by low fertility: "The decline of the French Navy was more severe than in other countries. Under the influence of population aging, the French Government and Parliament subsidized the Navy's sailing ships while other countries were adopting steam-powered craft" (1981, p. 234).

The U.S. Office of Management and Budget (OMB), the president's principal office for governmentwide planning and assessment, considered this matter in 1979 as part of a more general interest in the long-term implications of demographic change. The OMB analysis, published in the 1980 budget of the U.S. government, concluded that shrinkage of the potential pool of 18-year-old recruits need not cause any problems even for the all-volunteer armed forces, although recruitment rates among both males and females and retention rates of existing personnel would have to be increased (U.S. Office of Budget and Management, 1979). Similar analyses in West Germany led to comparable conclusions, as we note in the section on West Germany's responses to demographic change.

Demographic and Economic Significance of Immigration

The increasing demographic significance of immigration under conditions of low fertility, as outlined briefly in Chapter 5, is easy to understand. If domestic fertility declines, a constant absolute number of immigrants would account for increasing proportions of total population growth. If immigration numbers are raised to compensate for declining domestic increase, the proportional effect is magnified further. Only if immigration numbers are decreased in proportion to declines in native births will the proportion of growth accounted for by immigration not rise.

In countries with 0 or negative rates of domestic population increase (as would eventually occur in countries experiencing long-term replacement or below-replacement fertility), *any* level of immigration would account for *all* of whatever population growth might occur. Of course, at such low levels of domestic population increase, such a calculation can be misleading, since a very few immigrants could be said to account for 100% of growth (Teitelbaum, 1980, p. 42). As we have noted in Chapter 5, several industrialized countries may be in this position today.

Changing Population Composition with Low Fertility and Substantial Immigration

If absolute immigration numbers are substantial under conditions of slow or negative natural increase, there can be relatively rapid changes in the ethnic, racial, linguistic, or other social characteristics of the population. This is particularly the case if the immigrant streams come from social settings in which higher fertility levels prevail than in the country to which they migrate. Under these conditions, the compositional change caused by the immigration flow itself is heightened by the subsequent differential fertility behavior, even if (as is typical) the birth rate of high-fertility immigrant groups tends to converge downward over the long term toward the levels of the receiving country.

Bouvier and Davis (1982, Tables 3 and 5) have prepared projection simulations for the composition of U.S. population by "race," according to alternative assumptions about the levels of net immigration (see Table 6.1 and Figure 6.1).

Their projections assume only one trend line of fertility for each racial group. The total fertility rate for whites (non-Hispanic) is set at the recent level of 1.758 and is held constant. Asian and Other (native-born) fertility also is set at 1.758. Black (native-born) fertility

Table 6.1
TOTAL U.S. POPULATION, 1980–2080, BY ANNUAL LEVEL OF NET IMMIGRATION AND "RACE"[a]

Level and "race"	1980 No.	1980 %	2000 No.	2000 %	2020 No.	2020 %	2040 No.	2040 %	2060 No.	2060 %	2080 No.	2080 %
0.5 million immigrants/year												
White non-Hispanic	181.0	79.9	198.9	74.4	202.7	69.5	192.5	65.3	176.5	61.6	162.3	58.6
Black	26.5	11.7	35.2	13.1	41.7	14.3	44.6	15.1	44.6	15.6	43.2	15.6
Hispanic	14.6	6.5	23.8	8.9	32.4	11.1	38.4	13.0	42.3	14.7	44.6	16.1
Asian and Other	4.4	2.0	9.5	3.6	14.7	5.0	19.2	6.5	23.2	8.0	26.8	9.7
	226.5	100.0	267.4	100.0	291.5	100.0	294.7	100.0	286.6	100.0	277.0	100.0
1.0 million immigrants/year												
White non-Hispanic	181.0	79.9	200.3	71.7	205.6	64.9	196.9	59.0	182.4	53.9	169.5	49.8
Black	26.5	11.7	36.4	13.0	44.4	14.0	48.8	14.6	50.2	14.8	50.0	14.7
Hispanic	14.6	6.5	30.3	10.8	46.6	14.7	60.3	18.0	71.1	21.0	79.8	23.4
Asian and Other	4.4	2.0	12.1	4.3	20.3	6.4	27.8	8.3	34.6	10.2	40.8	12.0
	226.5	100.0	279.1	100.0	316.9	100.0	333.8	100.0	338.2	100.0	340.1	100.1
1.5 million immigrants/year												
White non-Hispanic	181.0	79.9	201.4	69.2	208.0	64.7	200.6	53.8	187.2	48.0	175.5	43.5
Black	26.5	11.7	37.7	12.9	47.1	13.8	53.0	14.8	55.1	14.1	56.8	14.1
Hispanic	14.6	6.5	37.3	12.8	61.8	18.1	83.1	22.3	102.1	26.2	117.6	29.1
Asian and Other	4.4	2.0	14.5	4.9	25.4	7.4	35.7	9.6	44.9	11.5	53.5	13.5
	226.5	100.0	290.9	100.0	342.4	100.0	373.0	100.0	390.0	100.0	403.4	100.0
2.0 million immigrants/year												
White non-Hispanic	181.0	79.9	202.1	66.8	209.4	56.9	202.8	49.2	190.2	43.0	179.1	38.3
Black	26.5	11.7	38.5	12.7	48.9	13.3	55.6	13.5	59.2	13.4	61.1	13.1
Hispanic	14.6	6.5	44.9	14.8	78.6	21.4	109.6	26.6	136.3	30.8	159.2	34.1
Asian and Other	4.4	2.0	17.2	5.7	31.0	8.4	44.3	10.7	56.3	12.7	67.5	14.4
	226.5	100.0	320.6	100.0	367.9	100.0	412.3	100.0	442.0	100.0	466.9	100.0

[a]In millions. Percentages do not always sum to 100.0 due to rounding. Source: Bouvier and Davis (1982, Tables 3 & 5).

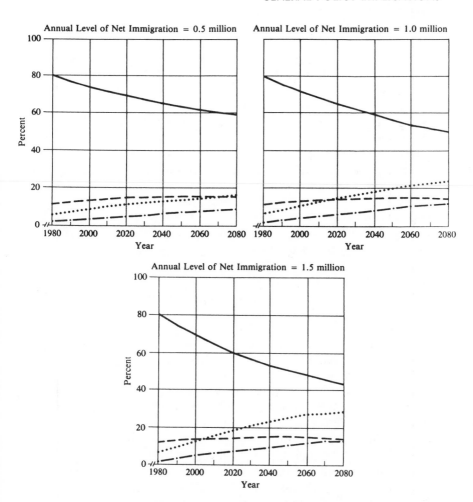

Figure 6.1 Percentage distribution of the total U.S. population, 1980–2080, by "race" and annual level of net immigration for white non-Hispanics (——), blacks (--), Hispanics (. . .), and Asians and Others (-•-). (From Bouvier and Davis, 1982).

is set at 2.33. Black (immigrant) fertility is set at about 10% higher, at 2.57. Asian and Other (immigrant) is also set at about 10% higher than native-born, at 1.93. Hispanic (native-born) and Hispanic (immigrant) total fertility are set initially at 2.6 and 3.0, respectively. All fertility rates are assumed to converge toward the 1.758 level of native-born whites (non-Hispanic) and Asians and Others.

Bouvier and Davis also assumed one trend line of mortality for each racial group. Life expectancy of white (non-Hispanic) and Asian and Other is set initially at 69.8 and 77.7 years for males and females, respectively. Hispanic life expectancy is set initially at 67.5 and 75.6 years. Black life expectancy is set initially at 65.0 and 73.6 years. No distinctions are made between native-born and immigrant groups with respect to mortality. All expectations of life at birth are assumed to converge in 2080 at 76.1 for males and 85.0 for females.

It should be emphasized that these are only *projections* or simulations. They are not predictions or forecasts in any sense. Under assumptions of about 1 million immigrants per year with current composition, over the long term the percentage of the population who are white (non-Hispanic) would decline from about 80% in 1980 to about 50% in 2080. The black percentage would rise slightly from nearly 12% to nearly 15%. Meanwhile the Hispanic population would increase dramatically, from about 6% in 1980 to 23% in 2080, and the Asian percentage would grow from 2 to 12%. Under these assumptions, the Hispanic population would be larger than the black population by about 2010.

An alternative assumption of net immigration levels of about 500,000 per year leads to projections with slower, though still substantial rates of change in composition. Whites (non-Hispanic) would decline from 80 to 60%, blacks rise from 12 to 15%, Hispanics from 6 to 16%, and Asians from 2 to 10%.

All of the above projections are based upon the assumption that recent fertility levels continue, albeit with the higher rates of certain racial groups converging to the levels of the lowest, that of the white (non-Hispanic). Alternative assumptions could certainly be made, for example, increases in white (non-Hispanic) or black fertility, more rapid (or slower) declines in Hispanic fertility, and so on. If higher fertility levels were assumed for the native-born groups, the proportionate impact of any given level of immigration would thereby be reduced. Hence such alternative projection simulations can provide useful confirmation of the general point that the demographic significance of immigration is closely related to the levels of indigenous fertility and population growth.

Projections such as those described above have been criticized as stretching overly far into the future. A 100-year projection period, in this view, is so long that almost everything can change; hence such projections have little value and can be quite misleading. While there is some validity to this criticism, the long time spans characteristic of population change mean that long-range projections do have heuristic value as long as they are not mistaken for predictions or forecasts; they illustrate the consequences of gradual trends that can be perceived only in the long term. They do *not* tell us what will happen, but only the logical long-term implications of a given set of assumptions.

POLITICAL RESPONSES TO DEMOGRAPHIC CHANGES SINCE 1965

Since 1965 there has been a steady stream of comment on demographic trends and their implications. These comments have applied to measures to reverse the trends as well as to adapt to them. (See the section entitled "Policies Affecting Fertility and Population Growth" in Chapter 7.)

Efforts to Reverse Declining Fertility

The most dramatic measures aimed at reversing fertility declines were enacted in Eastern Europe during the late 1960s and early 1970s, when both positive and negative measures were taken to raise the birth rate. The positive measures typically took the form of raising the economic incentives and lowering the costs of increased childbearing, coupled with the dissemination of propaganda aimed at encouraging the desired behavior. The negative measures typically restricted access to fertility control methods, the most extreme case being that of Rumania, discussed in Chapter 5. The Soviet Union was a laggard in this arena, adopting new pronatalist measures only in 1981. Again as we have seen, this reluctance was in part a consequence of political sensitivities arising from the simultaneously low fertility of the Slavic majority and the high fertility of the Muslim minority (Feshbach, 1982, p. 4).

In the West, pronatalist measures have been slower to arise and more muted and subtle, for several reasons. First, fertility declines to below-replacement levels lagged at least a decade behind those of Eastern Europe. Second, Western political traditions tended to limit state intervention in family matters, especially in view of the continued influence of organized religion. Third, the more pluralistic political systems of the West tended to place greater constraints upon controversial actions by governmental elites than in Eastern Europe. Fourth, the higher standards of living in the West meant that economic incentives to childbearing proportionate to those taken in Eastern Europe would be far more costly. Finally, the economic crisis of the 1970s constrained governmental action regarding low fertility in a way that might not have occurred in the preceding decade.

Nonetheless, it is undoubtedly still true that measures encompassing pronatalist elements have been adopted in the West. These have been concentrated in the field of welfare provision, most particularly in the levels and progressivity of family or child allowance provision. In 1982 in West Germany, for example, the child allowance per month for the first child was only DM 50; while that for the second child was DM 100; for the third, DM 220; and for the fourth and higher order, DM 240. Hence the parents of a single child received only DM 50, while those of three children received DM 370 (McIntosh, 1983, p. 210). Such progressive structures of transfer payments often have been justified with arguments that the incremental costs of the additional child are greater than those for previous children (a dubious assumption in most cases), and that larger families tend to be poorer and hence such measures have attractive redistributional effect. Whatever may be the validity of these claims, such family policies also appear designed to encourage larger families.

Efforts to Adapt to Low Fertility Trends

The consequences of the post-1965 baby bust were felt initially in the age-related social services dealing with the young: maternity wards first, then pediatric services, then primary and secondary schools. Each of these sectors felt the pressures of contracting demand in turn, and each responded depending upon the nature of its financial and political supports.

Almost all Western nations have registered a relative contraction in the size and funding of their regular maternity and pediatric services, whether their health systems are centrally planned or financed primarily via private health insurance. However, the decline in birth numbers has coincided with improvements and increased investment in perinatology, that is, the application of modern (and usually highly expensive) medical technologies to the treatment of premature or at-risk births that previously would have resulted in infant mortality or stillbirth.

With a lag of about 5 years, the decline in numbers (or at least the decline in the rate of increase) affected the early years of primary education. In most settings, the early tendency in the 1965–1984 period was to resist school closures, staff redundancies, and other adaptations, often out of inertia, but also due to the political power of the education lobby and the reluctance of many parents to lose their nearby primary schools. However, the realities of smaller numbers became quite evident over time as small schools declined further in size, and ultimately education authorities moved toward closures, reduction of teacher training programs, and the like. In nations with traditions of local control over education, these measures often generated passionate debate and community tension, with the result that contraction in educational resources often lagged behind the reduction in demand for them.

By the mid-1970s, once the new and unexpected fertility trends had been inserted into long-range projections, it began to dawn on Western governments that the assumptions built into their pension or social security systems might not be tenable over the longer term. Most of these systems are based on a pay-as-you-go taxation representing an intergenerational transfer from those of working age to those past a conventional retirement age. Notwithstanding the impression fostered by many governments, the working population is not paying into a fully funded pension system from which it will eventually be entitled to an annuity, as in a private annuity system. In fact, none of the governmental pension systems is fully funded in this sense, and all depend ultimately upon the capacity of the government to raise sufficient taxes on a continuing basis. With ever-larger cohorts of working age, a funding strategy is easier to sustain than with cohorts of stationary or even declining size.

Most government actuaries had assumed (often implicitly) that fertility would continue at replacement or higher levels, thereby generating a youthful age structure. This could allow for generous and increasing pension provision, declining age of retirement, and full indexing of pensions for inflation without imposing an unacceptable burden of taxation upon future generations of working age as they increased in size. But with fertility levels at or below replacement level, such provisions became fiscally untenable.

This debate became most heated indeed in the United States, where during the 1960s the real value of social security entitlements rose, and at the same time the effective age of retirement fell, while life expectancy at older ages rose considerably. Both the Carter and the Reagan administrations grappled unsuccessfully with the consequences, and a stopgap measure was adopted in 1981 to allow internal borrowing among the several social security trust funds. But by then it was clear that longer-term reforms were needed, and in December 1981 a bipartisan National Commission on Social Security Reform was established to fashion a political compromise. This commission issued its report in January 1983, and within a few months legislation was enacted embodying many of its recommendations. These included (U.S. Department of Health and Human Services, Social Security Administration, 1983b) (1) enforced social security participation for employees of federal, state, and local governments and nonprofit organizations (previously allowed to opt out); (2) delay and delimitation of cost-of-living increases; (3) taxation of social security benefits paid to people with higher-incomes; (4) higher social security tax rates; (5) a gradual increase in retirement age, from 65 to 67 over a 22-year period beginning in the year 2000. Of these revisions, the largest positive impacts upon social security finances were related to the retirement age changes, along with the decision to tax some social security benefits, as may be seen in Table 6.2.

As we shall note in Chapter 7, most industrialized nations will be compelled by the economic and demographic realities to face three options, either singly or in some combination: (1) to reduce retirement benefits in real terms, (2) to raise taxes substantially, or (3) to increase gradually the age at which pension rights become effective. The compromise proposals of the U.S. bipartisan commission embodies elements of all of these, but the most controversial was the gradual increase in pensionable retirement age. In effect, this represented a return toward pension conditions prevailing before the 1960s and was consistent with the increases in

Table 6.2

MAJOR LONG-TERM REVENUE EFFECTS OF 1983 U.S. SOCIAL SECURITY REFORM PROVISIONS[a]

Policy change	Net dollar revenue increase (loss) per $10,000 taxable payroll
Changing retirement age	68
Taxing social security benefits	62
Changing tax rate and credits	30
Shifting cost-of-living adjustments to calendar-year basis	30
Covering newly hired federal employees	28
Changing self-employment tax rate	23
Increasing delayed-retirement credit	(10)
Covering employees of non-profit organizations	10

[a]Source: U.S. Department of Health and Human Services, Social Security Administration, 1983a.

life expectancy at higher ages that have occurred since then (e.g., life expectancy at age 65 in the United States has increased from 12.9 years for males and 16.2 for females in 1965 to 14.0 years for males and 18.4 years for females in 1978 (U.N. Statistical Office, 1982, Table 34). Yet even discussion of future increases in retirement ages was particularly controversial during a period of high unemployment, as it slows the departure of older workers from the labor force. In addition, attention had to be paid to the likely increases in disability rates that could be expected to result from an increasing age of retirement, and appropriate provision had to be made to deal with such developments. We shall return in the concluding chapter to this vexing question of fertility decline and the provision of pensions.

THE POLITICS OF POPULATION IN FRANCE AND WEST GERMANY SINCE 1965

So far in this chapter, we have considered general policy questions facing all developed countries in light of the post-1965 fertility decline. It may be useful to provide a somewhat more precise picture of the political context of recent policy discussions in two countries with a long and checkered history of concern about population decline. Recent developments in France and Germay once more highlight the extent to which the matters raised in this book go far deeper than the administrative and technical, touching sensitive and important political issues likely to cloud and complicate present and future policy debates.

France

Huss has reviewed evidence of renewed concern about low fertility in France in the period 1974-1980.[1] Her survey of public statements by political leaders of all persuasions, by the media, and by various interest groups "showed a near consensus in deploring the present trend in fertility and in calling for state intervention, with more or less faith in its probable effects" (p. 67). Meanwhile, French public opinion did not reflect the same degree of anxiety expressed by the political leadership, resulting in the reluctance among some politicians to *appear* pronatalist, despite their sympathies.

Huss divided the views of prominent public figures into four groups: (1) active pronatalists, (2) moderate pronatalists, (3) those who consider themselves to be neutral but nonetheless express concern about low fertility, and (4) Malthusians. The first category, "active pronatalists", are really extreme pronatalists. They must be distinguished from active but "moderate" pronatalists, who are reluctant to be identified as such "because of the militaristic and repressive connotations of the word on the contraception and abortion issues".

One of the most visible active pronatalists has been Michel Debré, prime minister under Charles de Gaulle and one of the principal authors of the Constitution of the 5th Republic. Debré has revived the arguments of the late nineteenth and early twentieth centuries in speaking of "the demographic struggle" (*la bataille démographique*). In the National Assembly he has frequently

---

[1]The following discussion and quotations are based largely upon Huss (1980), especially pp. 27–44 and 67.

stressed the need to raise the birth rate, and his pronatalist views have been adopted as policy by the principal Gaullist party, the Rassemblement pour la République. Other smaller parties openly share this perspective, for example, Centre National des Indépendants et Paysans (CNIP) and the Mouvement des Démocrates led by Michel Jobert.

Among prominent intellectuals, some are also willing to express explicit pronatalism. The most prominent of these are the historian Pierre Chaunu and the demographer Alfred Sauvy. Chaunu's prose on the subject is full of hyperbole. To him contraception and abortion are "the White Plague" *(la peste blanche)*. "The new arsenal against conception and childbirth," he stated, is "infinitely more dangerous than atomic armaments" (quoted in Huss, 1980, p. 28). Chaunu has described contraception as "diabolical" and "genocidal," and as an organized conspiracy in which (as Huss paraphrased him) "the United States uses Europe as a guinea pig for profit motives. He even poses as a gynaecologist to explain how the pill, the coil and abortion bring about cancer, heart failure and other ills" (pp. 28–29).

Sauvy is one of France's most distinguished demographers, formerly director of the INED and now a respected professor of the Collège de France. He has published extensively on the implications of demographic change for slow economic growth, unemployment, and inflation in industrialized societies, and typically has argued that all could be improved by higher fertility rates. Sauvy has frequently referred to the earlier decadence of Athens and Rome, and has employed images of retribution: "So fundamental are the problems of population that they will take terrible revenge upon those who ignore them" (p. 30). We have noted these views in Chapter 2. Meanwhile, Sauvy argued, the rejected third child will "take his revenge" and the generations "which refuse to ensure their posterity" will suffer (p. 30).

Chaunu and Sauvy both are prominent members of the Association for a Demographic Renaissance (APRD), founded in 1976 to promote increased fertility. In its publications, the APRD employs highly emotive language:

> "cradles" and "coffins" replace "births" and "deaths," the desire not
> to have a child becomes "le refus de la vie" (the refusal of life), the de-

clining birth rate is a "cancer," *"la mort 'voulué,' totale et collective"* [the death wish, total and collective]. [Huss, p. 29; translations added].

To turn to the second category: The "moderate pronatalists" form a broader and more varied grouping, including those who agree with the "active pronatalists" but do not wish to be so labelled and those who wish to raise fertility only modestly, for example, to replacement level. Much of the political alliance that brought former President Giscard d'Estaing to power (the so-called Union pour la Democratie Française) took this view, and therefore opposed the "Loi Veil" (named for Simone Veil, Minister of Health) that legalized abortion in 1975. This law was enacted through the combined support of the Socialists and Communists.

President Giscard himself made many speeches on family and demographic issues. In 1978 he stated that "a society no longer capable of assuring the replacement of generations is a condemned society" (from *Le Monde*, in Huss, p. 33). In a 1979 television interview, he ranked demography among the four great issues facing France, along with the economy, Europe, and defense. Giscard even issued a presidential order providing a special cash payment of Fr 10,000 (which was popularly described as the "gift of a million" on the basis of the old franc) to couples giving birth to a third, fourth, or higher-order child (Huss, personal communication, July, 1983).

Within the Parti Socialiste of President Mitterand, some elements embrace this moderate pronatalist view. The president himself (before his election) even agreed publicly with some of the views of Michel Debré: "I certainly do not agree with all the proposals of M. Michel Debré, but he is right to affirm that a pronatalist policy must constitute one of the axes of governmental action" (translated from Huss, pp. 34–35). The present trend, if continued, would "aggravate the [process of] aging, and in the long run condemn the population to disappear" (p. 35). Jacques Delors, the minister of economy and finance in the Socialist government, has advocated a complete rethinking of government family policy and dismissed the reluctance to consider overt pronatalism as "old taboos that paralyze all action" (p. 35).

The third category, those who are "neutral" about pronatalist policies while nonetheless expressing some concern about low fertility, include the principal Marxist political groups—the Communist party and the Union Confédération Genérale du Travail—as well as the leading demographic research institution, the INED. In the Marxists' view, fertility decline is "demographic disequilibrium" that should be corrected. But they have asserted that the demographic problem is merely a symptom of a general crisis of capitalist France, which requires for its solution a fundamental political change that would restore fertility as a by-product. Once again, these are echoes of socialist views expressed in the interwar years. (See Chapter 3).

The INED as an institution takes no official position on pronatalism, in keeping with its scholarly status. However, many of its self-initiated research projects are in the field of fertility decline, and studies commissioned by the government frequently discuss the efficacy of alternative measures to raise fertility. In addition, the usually cautious reports of INED are occasionally reported in the popular press in more extreme and emphatic form.

The final grouping, the Malthusians, have a somewhat peculiar perspective in the French case, since no prominent political spokesman favors the reduction in French births. Instead, the Malthusian category is comprised of those who are totally unconcerned about the fertility decline or even welcome it. These are to be found among the ecologists, who find political favor among only 1–2% of the electorate.

Meanwhile, nonelite opinion (i.e., public opinion), as represented in polls conducted by INED, showed a gap between elite and public concern, but a gap that over the 1970s tended to narrow in the direction of support for higher fertility. It is still an open question whether any French government can command sufficient public support to finance subsidies large enough to affect fertility decisions.

That a future government may well try to reverse current demographic trends cannot be discounted. In an interview with the Parisian daily newspaper *Libération* of 30 October 1984, the Mayor of Paris and prominent right-wing politician, Jacques Chirac, provided a telling reminder of the persistence of the French fear of population decline. To Chirac, "Two dangers stalk French society: social democratization and a demographic slump." It seems we are back where we were during the turbulent days of the Third Republic (see Chapters 2 and 3). Furthermore, Chirac added that "If you look at Europe and then at other continents, the comparison is terrifying. In demographic terms, Europe is vanishing. Twenty or so years from now, our countries will be empty, and no matter what our technological strength, we shall be incapable of putting it to use." To prevent this from happening, Chirac advocated tax and abortion reform. And as his predecessors on the European right had done in the interwar years, he mixed these views with a reaffirmation of French nationalism, in this case in the form of a sharp attack on Arab immigration to France at a time of high unemployment (Chirac, 1985).

Future political developments are, of course, impossible to predict. But if we keep in mind the fact that Chirac is a likely candidate for the French presidency in the 1986 elections, we can see the extent to which the rhetoric of concern over population questions is very much alive and well in present-day France.

West Germany

Recent fertility levels in West Germany have been lower than in France—perhaps the lowest in the world. Whereas the period total fertility rate in France went no lower than 1.81 and as high as 1.97 over the past decade, in West Germany the decade's low was 1.32 and the high only 1.46 (see Appendix A). Yet there have been far fewer expressions of pessimism about the future or calls for pronatalist measures in Germany than in France.

McIntosh reported that German government officials and academics she interviewed in 1978 were concerned about demographic trends, but the goal of most of her respondents was limited: not to reverse the population decline, nor even to bring fertility levels up to replacement, but rather to slow the rate of population decline.[2]

Demographic discussion among intellectuals is also far more limited in Germany than in France. In part this reflects the continuing and unique force of the French cultural tradition of demographic debate, but in greater measure it results from recent German history and from the related weakness of German demographic re-

[2]The following discussion is based largely upon the work of McIntosh (1983), especially Chapter vi.

search, which fell into "disrepute" as a result of Nazi population policies. As McIntosh (1983) has suggested,

> For many years after the war, demographic research and population policy were identified with the Third Reich, and even mention of these topics prompted strong negative reactions. Demographic training was in eclipse; and as late as 1974, Herman Schubnell could write that there were only two university professors of demography in the entire Federal Republic, and no university-based population research institutes existed. (p. 194)

There is virtually nothing, then, in recent German literature to match the pronatalist writings of Chaunu, Sauvy, and others in France.

Within the powerful bureaucratic leadership of the federal ministries, concern about German's low fertility was also limited. The director of a federal Ministry of the Interior project on low fertility reported that there was no official view on the subject in the Ministry of the Economy. This was because the ministry's economists believed that population size is a relatively minor factor in economic growth, the more decisive factor being increased productivity per worker. Ministry economists also emphasized the importance of trends in world trade and West Germany's lack of indigenous energy and other resources. Ironically, McIntosh (1983) cited a French analyst, Chesnais, as an outside observer who fears "that the real problem is that labor shortages and rising costs will price German—and European—goods out of the market" (p. 186).

Apart from German sangfroid regarding economic issues, there has been some discussion of the implications for the social security system of changes in the population age structure. Social security taxes amounted to 18% of personal income in 1978, and with unchanged retirement policies and fertility levels would have to rise to 24% at the turn of the century. As a result, the possibility of allowing more flexibility for later retirement has been raised.

The issue of the future sufficiency of military manpower has also been discussed, albeit with great caution given sensitivity in West Germany to echoes of her military past. The Ministry of Defense held that "the base population of draftable age would be insufficient after about 1992 to provide, under present recruitment practices, for the needs of the armed forces" (McIntosh, 1983, p. 189). However, the likely focus of attention should such a problem arise may well be upon present military service practices, which currently allow draftees a wide range of alternative forms of service.

There is, however, one aspect of German fertility trends that has generated widespread concern: the juxtuposition of low German fertility with the high levels of foreign immigration and the much higher levels of fertility among these immigrant populations—a subject previously discussed in the section entitled ''Trends in International Migration'' in Chapter 5. The policy of guest-worker importation was initiated during the 1950s and accelerated in the 1960s, especially after the substantial closing of migration from the East with the building of the Berlin Wall. The high-water mark was reached in 1970, when net immigration of over 500,000 was registered. The guest-worker policy was subsequently cancelled in 1973, but reunification of families continued, and this, in light of the higher fertility of immigrant groups and the sharp declines in fertility among Germans in the 1970s, led to a continuing increase in the proportions of the population of foreign origin.

These trends must be set against the backdrop of rising unemployment and other economic problems of recent years. This combination has generated heated political and intellectual debate in Germany, in sharp contrast to the relative silence among German academics in earlier years.

In 1982, the ''Heidelberg circle,'' a group of 15 prominent German professors and scholars from many disciplines, issued a document on the subject that the press named the ''Heidelberg Manifesto.'' The document (reproduced in full as Appendix E) calls for the preservation of Germany's language, culture, and national character against the joint consequences of low native fertility and continued high immigration. However, given the sensitivity of such issues deriving from the Nazi past, the circle specifically rejected ''ideological nationalism, racism, and the extremism of the Right and Left'' (see Appendix E). The authors pointed out that the German ''birth rate is now barely one-half the rate needed to ensure the continued existence of our nation'' and that coupled with continued immigration ''many Germans are already strangers in the places where they live and work'' (Appendix E). However, they made no call for higher German fertility, relying instead upon ''concerted development assistance to improve the living conditions of the foreign workers in their native countries—not here in our country . . . [and for] the return of the foreigners to their native lands.''

The parallels with opinions recently expressed by Jacques Chirac are unmistakable. What both suggest is that it is wrong to dismiss such opinion as marginal. Indeed, in light of the discussion in Chapters 2 and 3, we can conclude that with different emphases and in different forms, the fear of population decline has been an integral part of demographic debate in Europe and America for at least a century, and is likely in different ways to remain so in the foreseeable future. A consideration of future trends and responses must bear this fact in mind. It is to this task that we turn in our concluding chapter.

Conclusions 7

ALARUMS AND EXCURSIONS

As we have seen, population decline—however defined—has evoked fear, confusion, and misunderstanding among a broad community of politicians, scientists, churchmen, and novelists in many different countries. The concern is by no means new, but instead it stretches back at least a century and has revived over the past decade. This final chapter summarizes the beliefs and sentiments that have been expressed about population decline, discusses plausible population projections, and looks at the policy alternatives to deal with a declining population should it occur over the next generation.

Perceptual Distortions Based on Historical Experience

The first, and perhaps most fundamental, source of fear of population decline is perceptual. The last quarter of the twentieth century reasonably may be seen as the tail end of 200 years of sustained population growth. Whatever its origins, demographic change was associated with all the massive upheavals of the industrial revolution. Consequently, we should not be surprised that population questions have become entangled with all the major political and social issues of the past century. Furthermore, it is understandable that the relatively new demographic patterns of this period came to appear to contemporaries as the natural order of things.

Continuing population growth is as characteristic of the past two centuries as is economic advance and technological progress. In virtually no case has a population declined or not grown for any sustained period, including times of severe duress during the two world wars. It should not be surprising therefore, that population growth has come to be considered normal in the industrialized world, and explicitly so, for instance, by the government of Rumania, as indicated in Chapter 6 and Appendix B. Conversely, nongrowth of population is bizarre and disturbing, and decline of population a positive threat—a reversal of the tide of nearly the whole of relevant history. Similar statements could be made about economic growth since the Second World War—growth is normal, slow-or-no-growth disturbing, and decline of a more than temporary nature highly threatening.

The importance of such perceptual differences may be illustrated by considering reactions to small population growth rates of, respectively, positive and negative sign. The small positive growth rate (say, $+0.3\%$) is normal and surely unthreatening, even to most of those concerned about rapid population growth, resource depletion, environmental degradation, and the like. However, a similarly small negative growth rate (-0.3%, for consistency) is commonly seen as a serious threat to the long-term viability of a nation, ethnic group, or culture. Only a few fringes of the environmental movement see such negative growth as desirable.

In demographic terms, however, population growth rates of $\pm 0.3\%$ do not differ markedly from one another. Both lead to modest population change, in opposite directions of course, over very long time periods. It takes 230 years for such populations to double or halve in size. Both result in modest distortions in age structure from those of a stationary population; in the positive growth case, the distortion is toward a somewhat more youthful population; and in the negative growth case, toward an older population. Over the very long term, both positive and negative growth rates are unsustainable. In the positive growth case, the population would grow to infinite size in finite space, which is a logical impossibility. In the negative growth case, the population would eventually cease to exist, but this could occur only over many centuries, given the slowness of the rate posited.

Of course, positive and negative growth rates of greater magnitude than the arbitrary $\pm 0.3\%$ discussed here are quite plausible, as is evident from some past and current trends as well as from low variant projections into the next century for Western Europe, and especially for West Germany (see the discussion of West Germany in Chapter 6). Population decline at such rapid rates would inevitably have more serious policy and political implications.

Misinterpretations of Population Projections

Related to these perceptual issues is the uninformed and/or misleading application of population projection techniques. Because population change in most industrialized countries is relatively slow, and because of the momentum of growth generated by higher fertility levels in the recent past, one must project far into the future to demonstrate empirically a perceived threat of substantial population decline. The problem with this approach is that no one can predict the actual course of fertility very far into the future in societies in which most couples control their fertility effectively.

Notwithstanding this limitation, those concerned about population decline have on occasion assumed continuing low fertility levels well into the next century to demonstrate empirically the threat of population decline they perceive. There is nothing wrong with this kind of projection as an illustration of long-term demographic implications, since an assumption of continuing low fertility is within the realm of plausible futures. However, fairness and caution would require simultaneous alternative assumptions involving, for example, modest increases in fertility to above-replacement levels, such as those that have occurred in recent years in Eastern Europe. Only through such alternative assumptions could plausible alternative futures be reasonably bracketed. But such an approach would also serve to weaken the case of those who fear population declines in the future.

Ideological Elements in the Fear of Population Decline

Ideological issues frequently spill over into concerns about population decline; indeed some belief systems inevitably determine their adherents' attitudes to the matter. This is not to say that ideologies remain static in face of changing demographic circumstances, for some important political and religious groups have demonstrated a remarkable flexibility on this issue over the past several decades.

One example is the turnabout on fertility questions in Eastern Europe and the Soviet Union. In the late 1960s and early 1970s, nearly all of the Warsaw Pact states of Eastern Europe became alarmed at the prospect of population decline. Since state intervention in such matters was politically legitimate, and since there were few political restraints on such action, all of these states took prompt steps to raise fertility. There was little attempt to conceal the pronatalist intent of the measures, since most were not inconsistent with Marxism-Leninism, even though entirely different responses had been derived earlier from the same ideological perspective.

A second ideological cluster concerned with population decline is that of conservative religious or nationalist groups. From the standpoints of these groups, population decline is seen as the demise of a valued moral or national order, and also diminishes the internal or international political power of the state, church, and/ or "race." Such people view the family as central to the nation and to religious traditions, and low fertility is seen as both cause and symptom of the weakening of the family by the secularism and moral relativism of modern society.

Religious conservatives often go further, to oppose one or all of the means employed to regulate fertility on theological and moral grounds. The most important example of this is the Catholic Church's opposition to abortion; in this they have been joined by some other conservative religious groups (e.g., fundamentalist Protestant and Orthodox Jewish). Moreover, these groups frequently express religious opposition not only to abortion, but also to most forms of modern contraception and/or sterilization, which they consider to be unnatural. Still, few religious denominations oppose all forms of fertility regulation, though the methods considered acceptable by the most conservative groups tend to be the least effective.

In recent years, such conservative religious perspectives have been given political impetus by the formation and vigorous action of the so-called right-to-life or pro-life groups. These groups have their origin in the Catholic Church's opposition to the liberalization of abortion laws in the late 1960s and early 1970s. However, as they have grown and prospered they have influenced other conservative religious groups, and their opposition has been extended to many forms of contraception and to measures aimed at changing the positions of women in society. Hence the opposition of most American pro-life groups to the Equal Rights Amendment.

A third ideological grouping includes some strange bedfellows who disagree on many issues but who are united by a common opposition to state intervention in individual fertility decisions. On one side are what may be broadly defined as libertarians. This group includes civil libertarians who oppose state restrictions on abortion and contraception and free-market libertarians who may oppose abortion and sometimes contraception, but on more general ideological grounds reject state prohibitions of these practices. On the other side of the spectrum are some feminist activists, who support state intervention in many respects (e.g., affirmative action, numerical quotas by sex, and legal requirements of equal pay for "comparable" work) but oppose state intervention affecting women's reproductive behavior, which feminists term "reproductive rights," or the "right of the woman to control her own body." Clearly, these views constitute deeply held political positions which inform many demographic discussions.

Demographic Differentials, Both International and Internal

Rates of population growth, whether positive or negative, are often compared to the rates of other groups. Within a country, comparisons are made between ethnic, racial, or religious groups. One nation's rate may be compared with its neighbors' or political adversaries'. Regional groupings may be compared, such as Western Europe with the third world. Broader (and sometimes quasiracial) categories are compared, such as European peoples as compared to Asian or African populations.

With regard to the international comparisons, we have noted in Chapter 5 that while high fertility rates have been declining in some countries of the developing world, the simultaneous decline of fertility in industrialized countries means that the differentials of this type are as wide as ever before experienced. Assuming that fertility declines in the developing world continue apace and that the low fertility of industrial nations does not decline still further, such gaps are likely to narrow over the coming decades, but the *perceptions* of quite gross differentials seem likely to persist. Described in this way, such differentials at international levels do arouse interest in some circles (see the discussion of M. Chirac's concerns in Chapter 6), but are sufficiently remote and theoretical as to fail to stimulate widespread interest.

The differentials become of far more general concern, however, when the reality or prospect of international migration is considered. As long as national differentials in population growth are contained within national boundaries, they evoke little anxiety in other nations. But if there is a pattern or prospect of large-scale migration from high-growth to low-growth nations, such national differentials become more visible and of greater concern in the receiving nations.

In this respect, international migration has now become an important point of intersection between the different demographic profiles of developing and developed countries. This is especially true today since in the past decades the nature of international migration has been transformed. Until the 1960s, international migration consisted largely of European out-migration to the New World or to overseas colonies. Since then, this pattern has shifted dramatically, so that now international migration consists overwhelmingly of movement from developing countries to industrialized or oil-exporting countries. Moreover, such migration is of large and increasing magnitude, and is of even greater proportional significance in industrialized receiving countries with rates of natural increase that are low to moderate and on a declining trajectory. Finally, the responses to migration are complicated by the fact that most of the migrants are defined as ethnically distinct (and often racially inferior) according to the social prejudices and mythologies of the receiving countries.

These factors together have tended to generate fears in the receiving countries that may be described as "nativist." Like the fear of population decline, such anxieties relate to absolute and relative numbers, rates of change in numbers, and projections far into the future. The anxieties involve concern both about future levels of in-migration in relation to natural increase of the native-born population, and about differentials in fertility between the "indigenous" population and the immigrants and their offspring. Since a large proportion of international migration now flows from developing countries with typically high fertility toward industrialized nations with low fertility, such fears depend in substantial part upon assumptions about future trends in fertility of immigrants and their offspring.

Such worries lead naturally to a discussion of differential population growth rates within nations or national groupings. These discussions take their most virulent form in settings in which one ethnic or religious group dominates others but is gradually being overtaken in size due to differential growth rates. A poignant example of this phenomenon is Lebanon. In the Constitution of 1937, principal political power was reserved for the then-largest group, the Maronite Christians, but differential population growth rates in the intervening period resulted in their becoming a minority by the 1960s. (The unwillingness of the Lebanese state to conduct a census since 1931 makes it difficult to know with any accuracy the magnitude of such proportionate shifts, though few would doubt that shifts did occur.) The Lebanese Civil War, which has been fought since 1975, is in large part over the reallocation of political control among the several antagonistic Lebanese communities, complicated and exacerbated by the long-standing Arab–Israeli conflict.

Within Israel, concern over the much higher levels of population growth among Israeli Arabs—growth rates of an exceptionally high magnitude—than among Israeli Jews, has led to a national policy that is pronatalist in intent, although the Israeli government has been careful to avoid even the appearance of limiting its pronatalist policies to the Jewish population. Meanwhile, some Arab nationalists encourage high fertility among the Arab population as a means of establishing eventual predominance over the Jewish–Israeli population.

In more subdued form, similar fears and actions may be observed in the Soviet Union. Population growth is low among the Russian and other European populations of the Soviet Union that have historically controlled its central political and economic institutions. At the same time, population growth is very high among the peoples of the Central Asian republics, which are non-European and overwhelmingly Muslim. This phenomenon has led to an extended debate within the Soviet elite as to whether there should be official policies aimed at stimulating population growth within the European nationalities, and if so how such policies can

7. CONCLUSIONS

avoid the reality or appearance of invidious pronatalism (DiMaio, 1981, pp. 151-179).

In Canada, there are evident concerns about the balance between the two major linguistic groups. A recent report of an expert meeting convened by the Canadian Government on demographic aspects of immigration noted that "the province of Quebec is more receptive to a policy encouraging childbearing than the rest of Canada," and pointed out that increasing immigration to compensate for low Canadian fertility presents the difficulty that in the past immigrants have resisted adoption of the French language (Canada, 1984a, pp. 5, 12).

A final example is provided by the debate in Great Britain over both Commonwealth immigration and of future demographic trends implied by the differentially high fertility of such immigrants and their offspring. The most vocal political figure on this subject has been Enoch Powell, member of Parliament, a conservative intellectual who in the 1970s raised the spectre of "black cities," of "streets of blood," and of other desperate consequences of demographic trends surrounding the influx and differential fertility of Commonwealth immigrants. Powell's warnings have represented only the most explicit statement of more widely shared concerns, and these have led to successive tightening of British immigration laws by both major parties since the early 1960s. While there have been several major legislative changes of this type, there has been no effort to affect the fertility behavior of immigrant populations, other than the provision of family planning service available to all through the National Health Service.

Economic and Social Welfare Elements in the Fear of Population Decline

Low population growth due to low fertility levels has traditionally fuelled doubts about the future adequacy of the labor force to staff the economy of industrialized societies, and especially of the number of young labor force entrants. There has also been related anxiety about the financial base needed to fund social services such as health, education, and housing, and to support retirement and services for the elderly. Groups such as the educational lobby and baby food companies also worry whether low fertility will have deleterious impacts upon the demand for the services they provide.

As we have seen, populations with low fertility and low population growth are characterized by a gradual aging trend that leads over several decades to increased proportions of the elderly and decreased proportions of the young. The most immediate effects of fertility declines are upon the size or growth rate of the latter group. In virtually every industrialized country, therefore, the demand for school places has declined, leading often to fractious debates about educational expenditure, about the closing of particular schools, and about employment prospects for teachers.

We have noted these difficulties in Chapter 6; they are likely to recur in the future. Such effects are most seriously felt in those few developed countries that experienced large-scale extended baby booms after the Second World War and that (however belatedly) invested heavily in the rapid educational expansion of the 1960s. In such settings, the effects of sharp fertility declines are heightened, for the recent decline in demand follows a period of rapid rather than moderate increase in supply. It also means that much of the hastily directed investment of the 1960s, both in physical and human capital (buildings, teacher training, etc.), has proven to be of only short-term utility; and in political terms it is far more difficult to justify the closing of a school completed at great expense in 1970 than of an antiquated structure built 50 years ago.

An objective observer might conclude that declining school enrollments ought to lead to proportionate declines in real expenditure on education. However, those involved in education argue otherwise, pointing out the deficiencies of the existing educational system, the need for greater attention to the smaller numbers of children, or the need for greater investment per capita because of the increased value of each child. Other credible arguments can and will be made against proportionate cuts in educational expenditure. Since fertility may prove erratic and could turn upward at any time, it makes good sense to avoid excessive cuts in expenditures. The practice of granting lifetime tenure to teachers means that sharp cutbacks will result in the loss of the youngest, best-trained, and perhaps most committed of the teaching profession. Proportionate cuts will lead to the loss of local schools in favor of more centralized institutions that are distant from the

7. CONCLUSIONS

neighborhood and require extensive and costly student transportation. Since the starting age of public education is arbitrary, it could be moved downward to provide early childhood education at a time when more mothers of young children are in the labor force.

At the opposite end of the age continuum, there is growing recognition that most government retirement or pension schemes are funded not through taxes paid over their working lives by the retired population, but instead by current taxation of the economically active population. As we have noted, such programs represent (and will continue to represent) resource transfers from one generation to another, mediated by government (see Chapter 6, p. 108). It is also now understood that if the size of the retired generation increases greatly in relation to that of the working population, the per capita tax burden will inevitably become excessive, unless the level of real benefits is decreased. There have now been fiscal projections of the implications of what the retirement of the postwar baby boom generations after the turn of the next century will mean. These have led to considerable alarm in some sectors about the actuarial soundness of national pension systems. Such worry is not without foundation.

However, several cautionary comments are in order here. First, some retirement systems have been indexed to inflation in such a manner as to result in pension increases that exceed real increases in wages of the working population. Continuation of this pattern long into the future would result in financial problems unrelated to changes in age structure.

Second, the age of retirement is itself quite arbitrarily defined, and modest and gradual increases therein can have surprisingly major impacts upon the long-term financial viability of the retirement program. In most countries the pensionable retirement age represents an accretion of amendments (usually downward) to arbitrary retirement ages established in the 1930s or earlier. The first such policy, that established by Bismarck in 1882, fixed retirement age at 70 years. European and American systems established in the twentieth century tended toward lower ages (e.g., 65), in part to encourage earlier retirement in order to provide jobs for younger workers in settings of high aggregate unemployment. Subsequent declines in retirement age resulted from political pressures during periods of economic growth and relatively high fertility.

Raising pensionable age is, however, not cost free (see p. 119). And as we have already noted in Chapter 6, while those in their 60s and 70s today have greater capacities to work than did older citizens in earlier years, policies leading toward increases in retirement age must allow for the costs of higher disability rates among this older working population.

Keynesian Economics and Population Growth

Declining fertility characterized the two major periods of economic crisis in this century: the depression of the 1930s, and the recessions of the mid-1970s to 1984. While no economist or demographer has been unwise enough to posit a clear causal link between recent demographic and economic trends, it was not surprising that some voices were heard advocating higher fertility as a stimulus to economic growth. Such opinions echo the earlier debates, in particular those relating to the under-consumptionist arguments of J. A. Hobson, and others relating to the source of economic difficulty for (and overseas expansion of) developed economies in the low consumption levels of their populations (Hobson, 1902; Lenin, 1947; and their epigone).

In a different and more influential form, John Maynard Keynes propagated the view that a higher birth rate would indirectly increase the marginal propensity to consume, and, through multiplier effects, increase the rate of investment and economic growth. Given Keynes' remarkable standing among economists and social administrators in the post-1945 period, it was inevitable that some economists would adopt a similarly pronatalist viewpoint, not primarily on the basis of political or ideological considerations, but in part because the Keynesian accelerator-multiplier model of economic growth seemed to work well when population growth was high. Despite the relatively recent assault by some professional economists, particularly the so-called Chicago school, on some of the assumptions on which the Keynesian system rests, Keynesian economics still influences some writing on population questions today. Unless there is a major upturn in the world economy in the

139

coming years, we should expect similar voices to be raised soon about the economic benefits of rising fertility (Petersen, 1955).

International Politics and Pronatalism

Centrifugal forces within the two major power blocs in the past decades have provided another set of reasons why pronatalist opinion may grow in the coming years. First, we must consider the increasingly independent stance taken in foreign policy by Western European states since the 1960s, when President de Gaulle developed the concept of an indigenous *force de frappe* (strike force) and withdrew France from the military structure of the North Atlantic Treaty Organization. This set of policy decisions played into the hands of those who, like de Gaulle, wanted to preserve France's political, economic, and cultural independence, and who saw in a rising birth rate a key to future national autonomy. The growth of anti-Americanism in other European countries could lead to a recrudescence of arguments that pronatalism and independence are inextricably related.

Second, stresses within the Soviet Union and the Warsaw Pact countries have also influenced the way those countries perceive population and related issues. Differential fertility rates between Muslim and non-Muslim populations within the Soviet Union have been noted in Chapter 5; these fertility rates probably underlie the security considerations of some Soviet planners about their southern border with Afghanistan and Iran, both deeply affected by the Islamic revival of the 1970s. Of course, there were many other reasons for the Soviet invasion of Afghanistan, but the reverberations of Asian events on the rapidly growing Muslim sectors of the Soviet Union should not be ignored.

Furthermore, the reassertion of Polish nationalism, with parallel (if muted) developments in virtually every Warsaw Pact state over the past two decades, provided an explosive mixture of older religious and anti-Russian sentiments. Pronatalist measures adopted in Eastern-bloc countries also have many sources, but no one who formulates social and economic policy in Eastern Europe can do so without a glance over the shoulder at the much more populous and powerful Soviet Union.

Policymakers are forced to confront most political issues at critical decision points. For example, whether to raise taxes or whether to deploy cruise or SS-20 missiles are issues that naturally come to a head and require decisive action. Population questions, however, have a much more subtle political character. Population trends are gradual and incremental in character, and in any case cannot be changed dramatically by any one set of policies. Hence, they normally do not command the attention of politicians harrassed by immediate political and economic problems such as inflation or unemployment, which are subject to rapid change and can be affected in the short term by specific fiscal or monetary measures.

In the mid-1980s, this tendency to postpone consideration of population questions has not gone unchallenged. As we have seen in Chapter 5, there have been attempts to mobilize the European Economic Community in support of pronatalist policies for Europe, and the American right has flirted with similar ideas, though it has not yet embraced them. Meanwhile, immigration policies have become politically explosive issues, very much on the current political agenda in the United Kingdom, the United States, and West Germany. But such matters have been eclipsed, at least partially, by the rise in international tension and the concomitant increase in the deployment of nuclear weapons in Europe. At times, the debate about East–West relations has dwarfed discussion of virtually all other political issues in Europe and elsewhere. Whether or not this will be the case in a few years remains to be seen.

PROJECTIONS OF PLAUSIBLE FUTURES

One of the most difficult problems in formulating appropriate responses to future fertility and population growth trends is in anticipating their likely form and magnitude. This may seem rather surprising, given the large investment made by most governments in collecting census and vital statistics data. The difficulty arises, first, from the primacy of fertility behavior over mortality trends in determining natural increase in developed countries, and second, from our inability to predict average fertility outcomes for the currently young cohorts that will account for the bulk of future fertility. The first of these should be self-evident on the basis of the discussion in Chapter 5; the second is methodologically more fundamental and therefore deserves elaboration here.

As has been noted in the discussion of period versus cohort rates in Chapter 1, it is cohort fertility that underlies the capacity of a population to replace itself. Unfortunately, given our inability to predict future fertility for women approaching or in the early years of childbearing, a cohort's lifetime fertility can be measured with reasonable accuracy only toward the end of its reproductive life. (Thus a demographic projection is easier to make for women in their late 30s and 40s, who have only a limited number of childbearing years left). This means that the last cohorts for which we can prepare plausible estimates are those born by about 1950, that is, those who bore most of the children they would ever bear before 1985. Moreover, since the 1960s marriage and first births have been deferred in countries such as the United States, and this factor has made the formulation of plausible demographic projections even more difficult.

The unavailability of comprehensible cohort measures for women with the greatest current fertility potential also means that most demographic measures on fertility are of the period form, that is, they seek to summarize the fertility behavior of women of all reproductive cohorts during a certain time period, usually a calendar year. While period rates, especially those that adjust for age structural differences (such as the total fertility rate, the gross reproduction rate, and the net reproduction rate) are of great utility, they are subject to distortions that can be quite misleading to the uninitiated. For example, it is well established in demography that with constant lifetime or cohort fertility, period fertility measures will increase with change toward earlier timing of childbearing, and decrease with the opposite change of delays in childbearing. Such a timing distortion was responsible in part for the scale of the postwar baby boom in the United States and elsewhere. The deferral of marriage and childbearing since the 1960s appears to have had the opposite effect—distorting downward the period fertility rates below the underlying cohort rates (see the discussion in Chapter 5).

While such effects are well understood by demographers, there is a danger that the levels and trends of period rates over a limited number of years will be misinterpreted by nonspecialists as indicating comparable changes in average childbearing for actual co-horts of women. While some downward change in cohort fertility surely has occurred over the past several years, its magnitude may be considerably smaller than that indicated by the trend in period rates.

To illustrate this difficulty, it is worth considering that in France from 1946 to 1966 the period fertility rates were consistently higher than the cohort fertility of every female cohort born during the preceding 100 years. From 1922 to 1935, in contrast, the period rates were declining while many of the cohort rates were actually increasing (Calot and Hecht, 1978, p. 181).

Several conclusions can be drawn from this discussion. First, since in the past decade there has been a significant change in the timing of fertility toward later ages, great caution should be exercised in drawing conclusions about eventual cohort fertility on the basis of the very low levels of period fertility evident in the annual data.

Second, those who fear that cohort fertility has declined to undesirably low levels must acknowledge that it is as yet too early to assess the long-term effects of timing changes on cohort fertility behavior. Given the slowness of these demographic phenomena, an observation period of a decade or more is not unreasonable.

Third, period rates in the coming years may prove to be far more erratic than in the past. The widespread access to effective means of fertility control means that for the first time nearly everyone can defer childbearing due to unfavorable temporary economic or social conditions. Ironically, the near universality of rational fertility control has sharply reduced our capacity rationally to predict collective fertility behavior.

With such caveats firmly in mind, it is instructive to consider empirically the implications of alternative high- and low-fertility assumptions upon medium-range projections, for example, up to the year 2025. Such projections have been prepared for each country and world region by the U.N. Population Division, and these projections are summarized for a selected set of developed countries in Table 7.1.

In preparing the projections, plausible assumptions are posited as to the levels of total fertility toward which each example might tend over the projection period. Net immigration is assumed

7. CONCLUSIONS

Table 7.I

PROJECTED DEMOGRAPHIC CHARACTERISTICS FOR HIGH- AND LOW- FERTILITY VARIANTS FOR VARIOUS DEVELOPED COUNTRIES AND FOR WESTERN EUROPE[a]

Population characteristics	Total fertility rates at 2020–2025[b]		Population projected in 2025 or in 2020–2025 interval		Estimated current characteristics (for 1980 or for 1980–1985)
	High	Low	High variant	Low variant	
United States	2.30	1.83			
Population (millions)			353.3	270.3	227.7
Age 0–14 (%)			22.4	16.9	22.5
Age 65+ (%)			15.5	19.6	11.3
Median age (years)			35.4	42.0	30.0
Annual population growth rate (%)			+0.83	+0.05	+0.86
United Kingdom	2.32	1.89			
Population (millions)			63.3	52.4	55.7
Age 0–14 (%)			21.5	16.1	21.1
Age 65+ (%)			16.3	19.7	14.8
Median age (years)			36.8	43.7	34.3
Annual population growth rate (%)			+0.35	−0.27	−0.01
France	2.30	1.89			
Population (millions)			63.3	51.7	53.8
Age 0–14 (%)			20.5	15.2	22.2
Age 65+ (%)			17.9	21.9	13.7
Median age (years)			38.3	46.1	32.5
Annual population growth rate (%)			+0.33	−0.28	+0.30
West Germany	2.34	1.61			
Population (millions)			61.3	48.2	61.7
Age 0–14 (%)			19.9	12.3	18.6
Age 65+ (%)			19.4	24.7	15.0

Table 7.I (*continued*)

Population characteristics	Total fertility rates at 2020–2025[b]		Population projected in 2025 or in 2020–2025 interval		Estimated current characteristics (for 1980 or for 1980–1985)
	High	Low	High variant	Low variant	
Median age (years)			39.7	50.5	36.6
Annual population growth rate (%)			+0.03	−0.91	−0.18
Western Europe[c]	2.30	1.75			
Population (millions)			165.1	133.4	153.8
Age 0–14 (%)			19.8	13.6	20.4
Age 65+ (%)			19.0	23.5	14.2
Median age (years)			39.6	48.5	34.4
Annual population growth rate (%)			+0.15	−0.60	+0.06

[a]Source: U.N. Department of International Economic and Social Affairs (1985).
[b]Net immigration is assumed to be zero, except for (1) the United States: net immigration of 750,000 per year through projection period for "high" variant, and 250,000 for "low" variant; (2) the United Kingdom: net immigration of −30,000 per year.
[c]United Nations category; includes Austria, Belgium, France, West Germany, Luxembourg, the Netherlands, and Switzerland.

to be 0 for all but the United States and United Kingdom. For the United States, constant net levels of 750,000 and 250,000 per year are assumed for the "high" and "low" variants, respectively. The zero immigration assumptions for France and West Germany seem doubtful, based on recent experience; and hence in this regard the United Nations' projections of population may prove to be on the low side.

As can be seen from Table 7.1, for all the summarized projections the high variant yields positive population growth of small-to-moderate magnitude. In all cases other than that of the United

7. CONCLUSIONS

States, this variant's growth rate in the years 2020–2025 is higher than that for the years 1980–1985.

For all but the United States again, the low-variant projection results in negative population growth (i.e., decline) of small-to-moderate magnitude. The decline rate of greatest magnitude in the period 2020–2025 is, unsurprisingly, that of West Germany at −0.91% per year. Meanwhile the U.S. low variant indicates continued positive growth of small magnitude.

It should be reemphasized here that both United Nations' projection variants assume 0 levels of net immigration for West Germany from 1980 to 2025. Given the large foreign population now resident in that country and the propensity of such populations to stimulate additional migration for purposes of family reunification, this assumption seems implausible, and hence the growth rates in the two variants are probably on the low side of plausibility. The zero immigration assumption for France and the "low" variant assumption for the United States also seem implausibly low, with similar implications for the projections.

The conclusions seem evident. Population decline of small to moderate magnitude seems possible for the larger developed countries in Western Europe by the end of the first quarter of the twenty-first century. At the same time, population growth of small to moderate magnitude is also possible for the same countries. No one can predict with any confidence the future course of fertility and net immigration to these countries, and hence it is impossible to choose between the possibilities of moderate decline versus growth. What does seem to be quite implausible from our current perspective would be positive or negative growth rates of more than moderate magnitude.

POLICY RESPONSES TO FEARS OF POPULATION DECLINE

Policies Affecting Fertility and Population Growth

Future policy responses to a fear of population decline can take at least four major forms: (1) measures to limit access to effective fertility control, (2) measures to increase fertility via incentives, (3) measures to increase immigration, and (4) the decision to adapt to demographic change rather than to influence it.

We have sketched the recent history of such policies in Chapter 6. It is clear that each of these approaches has its own set of costs and benefits. Few of these are subject to precise quantification; all touch sensitive ideological issues; each warrants detailed discussion.

Limiting Access to Fertility Control

Limiting the access of couples to effective fertility control has been an explicit demographic policy of a number of East European countries (especially Rumania since 1967). It has also been a policy with less explicit demographic intent in numerous states, particularly regarding certain methods. For example, abortion was illegal in most Western countries until the early 1970s; oral contraception is unavailable in Japan; some methods of contraception, abortion, and sterilization are illegal or restricted in Ireland; and sterilization is virtually unavailable in the Soviet Union. The effect of such measures, if applied in a draconian manner that leaves many couples few effective options for fertility control (as in Rumania and perhaps Ireland, but not in the other countries mentioned, where other options were freely available), is to increase the level of unwanted fertility and reduce the freedom of individuals to control their own fertility. (Teitelbaum, 1972, pp. 405–417).

In economic terms, the costs of increasing unwanted fertility may, in substantial measure, be borne privately as is usually the case with childbearing; however, it is possible for the state to compensate families for such increased costs through increases in family benefits. The costs in noneconomic terms of large numbers of unwanted children or in terms of individual rights and civil liberties cannot be quantified, but would appear to many to be substantial and significant in most countries where fertility control has come to be widely practiced.

Increasing Fertility through Economic Incentives

Measures to increase the levels of desired and realized fertility may be positive or negative in form: positive measures provide incentives for additional childbirths; negative measures diminish existing disincentives to such behavior. The positive type may take the form of birth bonuses, large child allowances, preferential ac-

147

cess to housing and other benefits for large families, early retirement or other such incentives for mothers of a defined minimum number of children, and so on. The negative type may take the benign form of either reducing the social and economic opportunity costs of childbearing (such as by widespread provision of child care facilities to maximize fertility among women desiring to work), or the harsher form of discouraging female labor-force participation so that such conflicts do not arise. The harsher alternative would not be attractive in most liberal Western nations, and would also present difficulties in most Eastern European nations, which have long experienced relative labor scarcity.

One interesting proposal that combines some aspects of the positive and negative forms has been put forward in France. Under this proposal mothers would receive a so-called maternal wage, calculated as one-quarter of the prevailing wage for employed women; this would serve as a financial incentive for childbearing and for departure of some women from the labor force, albeit voluntarily rather than coercively.

In Hungary the government offers families substantial discounts on the purchase price of apartments based on their commitment to bear defined numbers of children within a stated time span. In West Germany the level of family allowance provided for the fourth and fifth child is substantially higher than that for the first and second. In some East European countries, women are guaranteed 6 months paid maternity leave and the right to return to their jobs (David and McIntyre, 1981, ch. 5).

It is possible to estimate the costs of such proposals in different societies. Of course, where wages are high, as in most of West Europe and North America, incentives like those in Hungary would be very expensive. For example, the Hungarian provision includes, for almost all women:

1. a cash allowance for each child in family;
2. a uniform cash benefit upon childbirth (contingent on receipt of prenatal care) equal to more than 1-month wage for an average young female worker;
3. a paid leave from employment at full wage, lasting 5 months, at or following childbirth;
4. a flat-rate cash grant equal to about 40% of a woman's average

wage in addition to an unpaid but protected leave from work, until a child is age 3;

5. a specified number of paid sick days to care for a sick child at home as well as several paid personal leave days each year, all at close to full wage;
6. several special benefits in kind, including housing allowances, food and clothing grants (and subsidies), and scholarships.

The combined value of all these benefits, both for all children and for children under 3 years of age, has been estimated at 36% of the average total costs of childrearing (Kamerman and Kahn, 1981, pp. 45–46).

The costs of comparable measures in Western countries can be estimated roughly as follows (based on 1978 wages). To match the relative levels of family allowances provided for a three-child family in Hungary and Bulgaria (about 33–34% of average manufacturing wages) would require increasing the monthly family allowances to £110 in the United Kingdom (a 70% increase); to Skr 1375 in Sweden (a 120% increase); and to over DM 700 in West Germany (more than a 100% increase). If the even higher relative payments in Czechoslovakia were to be employed as a model for Western countries, the above estimated payments would increase by an additional 60% to £175 in the United Kingdom; Skr 2000 in Sweden; and DM 1135 in West Germany. (Estimated from data in Frejka, 1982, Table 2.)

As noted, all of the above are based on 1978 wage levels and would be considerably higher today if adjusted for inflation. Moreover, they exclude pronatalist incentives other than child allowances, such as listed above for Hungary. The conclusion is self-evident: Adoption by high-wage Western countries of financial incentives for childbearing that are comparable in relative terms to those of Eastern Europe will be a very expensive proposition.

Encouraging Immigration

Measures to increase immigration can also be adopted as a means to restrain population decline. Deliberate policies of encouraging immigration have been employed in the past century by countries including Argentina, Australia, Canada, France, New Zealand, and the United States. In a different form, other developed countries have recruited large numbers of workers who were envisaged to be temporary (*gastarbeiter*, "guest workers," in Germany and Switzerland), but in reality many such temporary migrants have become permanent. (See "Trends in International Migration" in Chapter 5 for a more complete discussion.) In 1984, there were arguments in Canada for increased admissions for immigrants and refugees due to "the decline in the birth rate [and] the prospect of an absolute decline in the Canadian population by the turn of the century." (Canada, 1984c, p. 1).

Immigration as a means of retarding population decline has its own unique limitations, since if it is substantial in size while the indigenous population is declining, it unavoidably leads to rapid changes in the cultural, racial, linguistic, or ethnic composition of the national population. Such dramatic changes in composition appear almost always to generate widespread and often passionate opposition, based on collective fears that may well be more powerful than the fear of population decline. (See, for example, Canada, 1984a, p. 15.) It seems doubtful, therefore, whether large-scale immigration can ever serve as a politically viable response to declining population over a considerable period of years, unless the immigrant streams are considered similar in character to the indigenous population (e.g., East Germans to West Germany; *pieds noirs* in France; Oriental Jews in Israel; Angolan colonials in Portugal).

Adapting to Demographic Change

Finally, doing little or nothing to affect low fertility or actual population decline may also be considered to be a policy, in this case one of adapting to changing demographic trends rather than trying to modify the trends themselves. Such policies would include

1. transforming excess educational capacity to other purposes, for example, converting surplus schools to flats or nursing homes;
2. modifying the terms of retirement to reduce real benefits or raise the age of entitlement to a government pension;
3. building in flexibility to physical plant and social institutions

so that they can respond to fluctuating cohort sizes, based on expectations of erratic period rates.

If, for example, year-to-year birth numbers fluctuate, it is possible to introduce compensatory shifts in the (arbitrary) age criteria for school entry by several months forward or backward. Meanwhile the training of primary and secondary school teachers can be changed to provide for alternative occupations should the demand for teachers decline, and the automatic provision of tenure to teachers after a few years can be modified or restricted to a basic core number, with a cadre of auxiliary teachers hired as needed on different terms. The changing needs of industry, of especial importance in a period of rapid technological change, can be met by greater availability of in-service retraining programs or by conversion courses at mid-career. Industries whose markets are heavily dependent upon the numbers of children can gradually diversify their business so as to be less vulnerable to fertility decline.

Summary

All these alternative responses involve costs, be they financial or political. However, for perspective, it is worth stating that such costs are likely to be modest when compared to those in other spheres of public policy, such as economic policies that generate high inflation rates or unemployment, foreign policies such as foreign aid or military assistance programs, or military policies involving large-scale investment in arms and personnel. Inaction may be politically attractive but carries with it the danger of postponing consideration of a problem that may not appear critical today, but that will vitally affect the world in which our children and grandchildren live.

The overall conclusion of the above analysis is that, in the medium-term future, caution and patience must govern policy responses to fertility trends. Above all, we must avoid replication of the errors of demographic forecasting in the 1930s, when a confusion between cohort and period rates contributed to the conclusion by some established scholars that, in the course of a century, the populations of some Western countries might virtually disappear. It is likely that period fertility rates will continue to be depressed for some time to come, even lower than the underlying cohort rates, and it is important that policy be informed by knowl-edge of the difference between the two.

Moreover, there must be increased understanding of the real demographic similarities, over the short to medium term, between populations registering small negative growth rates (say, of −0.3%) and those with small positive growth rates (say, of +0.3%). Also, the similarities should be understood between a population having just below replacement fertility, say of 1.9, and that of a population with a total fertility rate of 2.3. With such understanding, popu-lation policy need not take on the complexion of panic as it has in the past, and its formulation need not take place in an atmosphere of soul searching or anxiety over the future. As we have seen in Chapters 2 and 3, so many writers, politicians, and scientists have engaged in scaremongering on this subject that there is no reason to add to their number.

We have drawn attention not only to the ideological element in population debate over the past century, but also to the more rig-orous discussions of the causes of fertility decline since the Second World War (see Chapter 5). Some scholars have developed the view that there is likely to be a substantial fertility increase in the next decade, and while we have reasons to be skeptical of this predic-tion, it is certainly not an impossibility. Demographers ought to join Heraclitus in affirming that there is nothing permanent except change. To watch and wait seems the best counsel in discussions of population questions over the next decade.

If period fertility rates remain substantially below replacement levels (e.g., at the less than 1.4 children per woman registered by West Germany in 1983) or if they should decline further, it may be necessary in a decade or so to consider new policy initiatives. We have already described some of these options. On principle, we would oppose draconian negative measures, such as those taken in Rumania, aimed at restricting access to contraception or at ban-ning abortion. These are too extreme and divisive to form the basis for policy on this complex question. In contrast, positive incentives in the form of family allowances, extended maternity leave at full pay, tax relief, or housing subsidies may well provide an attractive way of reducing the opportunity costs of childbearing. We must be aware, however, of the major financial implications of these policies; in conditions of economic stagnation or instability, these positive measures may prove too costly.

Policies Affecting Retirement Benefits

Other financial questions will arise whether or not fertility rates move upward or downward in the coming years. We refer to the potential difficulty in securing the future financial basis of Western pension schemes. In roughly the year 2010, the baby boom generation will reach retirement age. Of course, in those countries that had boomlets, the problem will not take on a sudden or acute form. But given the fact that economic growth in Europe is, to an extent, a function of levels of American demand, we all must take account of the fact that the United States is one of the countries in which the full social, economic, and political consequences of the baby boom will emerge when the birth cohorts of 1947–1965 retire. Will there be sufficient taxpayers in the American labor force at that time to provide retirement benefits comparable to today's without an unacceptably high tax burden? If fertility levels were to remain low or continue to drop, the answer would likely be "no." Of course, tax receipts are a function of productivity and profit levels, which are very difficult to measure, let alone to predict. But it seems wise at least to entertain the possibility that economic difficulties will persist in the coming decades.

If this scenario were to be realized, what could be done? Five options can be identified; each is unattractive in some respects, but one or more might prove to be unavoidable. Recapitulating the arguments presented in the section in this chapter entitled "Economic and Social Welfare Elements in the Fear of Population Decline," let us consider each in turn:

1. Lowering retirement benefits. The first option is to reduce retirement benefits, either in monetary or real terms. Most political leaders would only do this reluctantly, or only in extremis for political reasons; namely, in recognition that the elderly have the vote and use it for increasing numbers of years after retirement.

2. Raising the age of entitlement to a government pension. The

second option is to raise the pension age, thus reducing the size of the pensioned group and increasing the tax-paying population. This could provide the necessary funding for those entitled to pensions, but in an era of persistent unemployment, which is particularly heavy among young workers, there are substantial costs attached to this option as well.

3. Increasing family allowances. The third option is the provision of financial or other benefits to reduce the disincentives of having a second or third child. If such measures were to be adopted, they would have to be substantial and take effect at least 20 years before the large baby boom birth cohort reaches retirement age.

4. Limiting or banning contraception and/or abortion. The fourth option is to raise fertility via coercive measures, for example, by banning access to contraceptive information and services, and/or by delegalizing abortion and prosecuting those providing and obtaining them. The costs of such actions, in terms of political and civil liberties, would be high in most Western countries.

5. Increasing immigration. The fifth option is to increase immigration to compensate for low natural increase. For such a policy to be effective, it must be structured to assure entry by young workers and their dependents while limiting entry of older dependents. Demographically, substantial immigration in the context of below-replacement fertility would imply rapid changes in the composition of the population, and hence the political costs of such a policy would likely to be high unless the in-migrating population was deemed similar in ethnic and cultural characteristics.

Under current circumstances, the most politically acceptable and least divisive approach would be based upon a mixture of options 2 and 3. Option 1, reducing retirement benefits; option 4, banning contraception and/or abortion; and option 5, increasing immigration, are likely to raise very substantial opposition in most Western countries. In spite of such political problems, the 1983 fiscal reforms in the United States reduced retirement benefits by taxing those of higher-income groups, and similar measures may be implemented elsewhere in the future. The advantage of options 2 and 3 is that they can be justified on grounds unrelated to the demographic questions raised in this book; the arguments for raising family allowances and the pension age, after all, have a logic of their own. Of these two options, option 2, concerning pensions, would likely meet most of the fiscal burdens implied by the retirement of the baby boom generation. Option 3, raising family allowances, would require very substantial financial commitments to have any significant effects upon fertility levels.

There are, of course, so many imponderables about the context—social, political, and economic—in which these decisions will be taken that it is futile to do more than outline the evidence, perceptions, and alternative choices that deserve consideration. This we have tried to do, in the belief that scholars must avoid perpetuating the fear of population decline. If this study furthers the discussion of fertility trends by identifying both their ideological and demographic implications, then its aim in large part will have, been realized.

Appendices

Appendix A: TOTAL FERTILITY RATES, 1920–1983[a]

Year	United States[b]	Soviet Union[c]	Japan	England–Wales	Scotland	Canada	France	Den-mark	Finland	Nor-way	West Germany	East Germany	Belgium	The Nether-lands
1920	3.22		5.26	3.09			2.64	3.18	3.71					
1921	3.28			2.70		3.52	2.58	2.99	3.53					
1922	3.07			2.45		3.40	2.42	2.83	3.37					
1923	3.06			2.39		3.23	2.40	2.83	3.39					
1924	3.07			2.29		3.21	2.34	2.75	3.16					
1925	2.95		5.16	2.20		3.13	2.38	2.62	3.12		2.21[h]			
1926	2.84			2.16		3.33	2.36	2.56	3.02		2.10			
1927	2.78			2.02		3.29	2.32	2.41	2.89		1.98			
1928	2.63			2.02		3.29	2.32	2.41	2.91		1.99			
1929	2.51			1.96		3.21	2.23	2.27	2.81		1.93			
1930	2.56		4.73	1.96		3.29	2.27	2.29	2.75		1.88			3.02[f]
1931	2.44			1.89		3.21	2.25	2.21	2.57	2.14	1.71			2.88
1932	2.36			1.83		3.09	2.23	2.21	2.44	2.04	1.62			2.87
1933	2.21			1.73		2.86	2.11	2.08	2.26	1.85	1.58			2.70
1934	2.30			1.77		2.82	2.15	2.15	2.32	1.81	1.93			2.68
1935	2.23			1.75	2.18	2.78	2.05	2.13	2.36	1.79	2.03			2.60
1936	2.19			1.77	2.20	2.70	2.07	2.15	2.30	1.79	2.07			2.60
1937	2.23		4.38	1.79	2.16	2.65	2.09	2.19	2.38	1.83	2.09			2.54
1938	2.28	4.42	3.82	1.85	2.22	2.70	2.13	2.19	2.50	1.88	2.25			2.64
1939	2.23		3.74	1.83	2.18	2.65	2.17	2.15	2.57	1.92	2.39		2.12[i]	2.66
1940	2.30		4.13	1.75	2.14	2.78	1.99	2.23	2.15	1.94	2.40		1.83	2.68
1941	2.40			1.73	2.18	2.84	1.84	2.25	2.89	1.83	2.25		1.67	2.60
1942	2.63			1.91	2.43	2.94	2.00	2.50	1.99	2.12	1.83		1.77	2.70
1943	2.72			2.02	2.39	3.05	2.15	2.66	2.44	2.25	2.00		2.06	2.97
1944	2.57			2.24	2.43	3.00	2.23	2.83	2.54	2.43	1.89		2.10	3.11
1945	2.49			2.04	2.24	3.00	2.29	2.97	3.04	2.43	1.53		2.16	2.95
1946	2.94			2.49	2.76	3.38	2.97	3.01	3.41	2.76	2.00		2.51	3.96
1947	3.27		4.52	2.70	3.09	3.60	3.01	2.89	3.47	2.64	2.03	1.69[j]	2.45	3.69
1948	3.11		4.38	2.39	2.72	3.44	2.97	2.70	3.47	2.54	2.08	1.69	2.45	3.38
1949	3.11		4.29	2.26	2.61	3.44	2.97	2.58	3.32	2.49	2.15	2.04	2.39	3.22

Year														
1950	3.09		3.62	2.18	2.53	3.44	2.93	2.60	3.14	2.49	2.10	2.35	2.35	3.09
1951	3.27		3.25	2.16	2.41	3.44	2.77	2.50	3.02	2.43	2.06	2.46	2.29	3.15
1952	3.36		2.98	2.16	2.43	3.64	2.73	2.54	3.06	2.56	2.09	2.42	2.33	3.09
1953	3.42		2.69	2.22	2.43	3.75	2.66	2.58	2.95	2.64	2.08	2.40	2.33	3.03
1954	3.54		2.47	2.20	2.49	3.85	2.69	2.54	2.85	2.68	2.13	2.38	2.37	3.01
1955	3.58		2.36	2.22	2.53	3.83	2.68	2.57	2.93	2.74	2.14	2.38	2.39	3.06
1956	3.69		2.20	2.36	2.63	3.86	2.67	2.59	2.91	2.83	2.23	2.30	2.43	3.06
1957	3.77	2.84	2.03	2.45	2.73	3.92	2.70	2.55	2.86	2.82	2.33	2.24	2.47	3.08
1958	3.70	2.82	2.10	2.51	2.79	3.88	2.69	2.54	2.69	2.85	2.32	2.22	2.51	3.11
1959	3.71		2.03	2.53	2.78	3.94	2.74	2.50	2.75	2.86	2.40	2.36	2.59	3.18
1960	3.65	2.82	1.99	2.66	2.88	3.90	2.73	2.56	2.72	2.84	2.37	2.35	2.56	3.13
1961	3.63		1.95	2.57	2.91	3.84	2.82	2.56	2.70	2.87	2.46	2.42	2.64	3.23
1962	3.47		1.95	2.84	2.99	3.78	2.79	2.66	2.64	2.88	2.44	2.42	2.59	3.19
1963	3.33	2.52	1.98	2.85	3.02	3.70	2.89	2.60	2.64	2.92	2.52	2.47	2.68	3.20
1964	3.21	2.46	1.89	2.88	3.07	3.54	2.90	2.61[d]	2.53	2.94	2.55	2.51	2.71	3.19
1965	2.91[a]	2.46	2.14	2.81	2.96	3.15	2.84[d]	2.62	2.47[d]	2.93[d]	2.50	2.48	2.61[d]	3.04[d]
1966	2.72	2.44	1.58	2.74	2.87	2.81	2.79	2.35	2.40	2.89	2.53	2.40	2.52	2.90
1967	2.56	2.41	2.22	2.63	2.84	2.59	2.66	2.12	2.32	2.80	2.49	2.33	2.42	2.79
1968	2.46			2.55	2.77	2.44	2.58	2.00	2.14	2.75	2.38	2.29	2.31	2.72
1969	2.46			2.45[d]		2.39	2.53	1.95	1.93	2.70	2.21	2.23	2.25	2.75
1970	2.48	2.39[e]	2.13	2.38	2.54	2.33[g]	2.47	2.04	1.83	2.51	2.01	2.19	2.24	2.58
1971	2.27	2.50[f]	2.15	2.39	2.28	2.22	2.49	2.03	1.68	2.49	1.92	2.13	2.21	2.36
1972	2.01	2.40	2.12	2.19	2.14	2.06	2.41	1.92	1.58	2.38	1.72	1.78	2.09	2.15
1973	1.87	2.40	2.12	2.02	1.98	1.96	2.30	1.90	1.49	2.23	1.54	1.58	1.95	1.90
1974	1.83	2.40	2.04	1.90	1.91	1.90	2.11	1.92	1.61	2.13	1.51	1.54	1.83	1.77
1975	1.77	2.41	1.89	1.79	1.80	1.90	1.93	1.75	1.68	1.98	1.45	1.54	1.73	1.66
1976	1.74	2.39	1.83	1.73	1.71	1.85	1.83	1.66	1.70	1.86	1.46	1.64	1.72	1.63
1977	1.78	2.37	1.78	1.68	1.75	1.82	1.87	1.67	1.68	1.75	1.41	1.85	1.71	1.58
1978	1.75	2.32	1.77	1.75	1.85	1.76	1.83	1.60	1.64	1.77	1.38	1.90	1.69	1.58
1979	1.80	2.28	1.74	1.86	1.84	1.76	1.87	1.55	1.64	1.75	1.38	1.90	1.69	1.56
1980	1.82		1.72	1.90	1.86	1.79	1.96	1.44	1.63	1.72	1.45	1.94	1.68	1.60
1981	1.81			1.80	1.73		1.97	1.43	1.64	1.70	1.44	1.85	1.66	1.56
1982	1.81			1.76			1.94		1.72	1.71	1.41	1.85	1.60	1.50
1983							1.81				1.32			

(continued)

Appendix A (*continued*)

Year	Bulgaria	Czecho-slovakia	Hun-gary	Poland	Rumania	Yugo-slavia	Sweden	Switz-erland	Austria	Italy	Australia	New Zealand
1920		3.28ʰ	3.80ʰ				3.20					
1921		3.45					2.91				3.10	2.96
1922		3.27					2.64				3.10	2.94
1923		3.16					2.52				3.02	2.80
1924		2.96	3.18				2.42				3.00	2.78
1925	4.83	2.82	3.36				2.31				2.96	2.74
1926	4.86	2.75	3.24				2.21				2.83	2.72
1927	4.28	2.58	3.05				2.09				2.79	2.64
1928	4.25	2.54	3.08				2.07				2.75	2.55
1929	3.89	2.43	2.92				1.94				2.63	2.47
1930	3.96	2.45					2.00			3.38	2.57	2.45
1931	3.69	2.32	2.84				1.86	1.93		3.21	2.34	2.41
1932	3.91	2.27	2.72	3.42			1.82	1.91	1.83	3.06	2.18	2.22
1933	3.59	2.09	2.57				1.69	1.89		3.04	2.16	2.14
1934	3.70	2.03	2.55	3.11			1.69	1.83		3.00	2.12	2.12
1935	3.27	1.95	2.48				1.67	1.81		2.98	2.12	2.08
1936	3.24	1.93	2.42				1.73	1.75		2.86	2.18	2.14
1937	3.04	1.95	2.46	3.02			1.76	1.79	1.54	2.94	2.22	2.20
1938	2.87	2.07	2.50				1.82	1.81		3.08	2.20	2.29
1939	2.68	2.30	2.47				1.88	1.83		3.10	2.22	2.37
1940	2.75	2.64					1.84	2.08		3.08	2.26	2.64
1941	2.72	2.57	2.48				1.90	2.30		2.73	2.36	2.82
1942	2.78	2.52	2.52				2.19	2.45		2.69	2.38	2.68
1943	2.66	2.75	2.40				2.42	2.51		2.55	2.59	2.38
1944	2.65	2.83	2.61				2.58	2.61		2.34	2.65	2.68
1945	2.88	2.78	2.37				2.60	2.65		2.32	2.75	2.92
1946	3.06	3.21	2.30				2.56	2.61		2.92	3.00	3.27
1947	2.84	3.10	2.54	3.29			2.50	2.65	2.30	2.84	3.06	3.46
1948	2.87	3.00	2.58				2.48	2.59		2.82	2.98	3.40
1949	2.86	2.89	2.54				2.37	2.57		2.61	3.00	3.34
1950	2.94	3.04	2.60	3.71ʰ		3.74	2.29	2.49		2.51	3.06	3.40
1951	2.45	3.02	2.53	3.75		3.29	2.21	2.56	2.03	2.36	3.06	3.38
1952	2.44	2.97	2.47	3.67		3.60	2.23	2.56	2.05	2.32	3.18	3.54
1953	2.41	2.87	2.76	3.60		3.38	2.27		2.07	2.30	3.20	3.50

Year												
1954	2.35	2.83	2.97	3.58	3.07[k]	3.36	2.17	2.40	2.11	2.36	3.20	3.62
1955	2.41	2.85	2.81	3.61	2.89	3.16	2.25	2.27	2.22	2.36	3.27	3.74
1956	2.36	2.84	2.60	3.51	2.73	3.02	2.27	2.30	2.41	2.38	3.30	3.79
1957	2.26	2.75	2.30	3.49	2.59	2.76	2.29	2.35	2.47	2.32	3.41	3.90
1958	2.23	2.57	2.18	3.36	2.43	2.77	2.24	2.33	2.53	2.28	3.42	3.98
1959	2.23	2.39	2.09	3.22	2.34[h]	2.74	2.22	2.37	2.59	2.35	3.45	4.02
1960	2.30	2.39	2.02	2.98	2.17	2.79	2.18	2.45	2.59	2.37	3.44	4.05
1961	2.28	2.38	1.94	2.83	2.04	2.73	2.22	2.49	2.79	2.42	3.54	4.18
1962	2.22	2.34	1.79	2.72	2.01	2.68	2.26	2.47	2.84	2.46	3.41	4.06
1963	2.19	2.50	1.81	2.70	1.96	2.66	2.32	2.69	2.83	2.53	3.34	3.82
1964	2.16	2.51	1.82	2.59	1.91	2.64	2.49	2.67	2.78	2.67	3.14	3.61
1965	2.08	2.37	1.82	2.52	1.80	2.71	2.42[d]	2.61[d]	2.68[d]	2.55[d]	2.97	3.34
1966	2.03	2.22	1.89	2.43	3.66	2.65	2.36	2.52	2.66	2.52	2.88	3.25
1967	2.28	2.09	2.01	2.33	3.63	2.56	2.28	2.41	2.63	2.48	2.85	3.22
1968	2.27	2.01	2.06	2.24	3.19	2.48	2.07	2.30	2.59	2.44	2.89[j]	3.17
1969	2.17	2.05	2.03	2.20	2.89	2.44	1.93	2.19	2.50	2.45	2.88	
1970	2.10	2.07	1.97	2.20	2.67	2.29	1.92	2.09	2.32	2.37	2.85[d]	3.17[d]
1971	2.03	2.12	1.93	2.25	2.55	2.38	1.96	2.03	2.21	2.41	2.85	3.17
1972	2.15	2.20	1.93	2.23	2.44	2.36	1.91	1.90	2.09	2.36	2.65	2.98
1973	2.29	2.37	1.93	2.24	2.71	2.30	1.87	1.80	1.95	2.33	2.40	2.78
1974	2.23	2.48	2.27	2.25	2.60	2.28	1.77	1.72	1.92	2.31	2.31	2.59
1975	2.24	2.44	2.35	2.27	2.56	2.27	1.68	1.61	1.84	2.19	2.14	2.37
1976	2.20	2.41	2.23	2.30	2.57	2.26	1.64	1.54	1.70	2.08	2.05	2.28
1977	2.15	2.36	2.15	2.22	2.52	2.19	1.60	1.53	1.65	1.95	2.01	2.19
1978	2.15	2.36	2.07	2.20	2.48	2.15	1.66	1.50	1.63	1.85	1.95	2.12
1979	2.05	2.33	2.01	2.25	2.43	2.12	1.68	1.52	1.62	1.74	1.90	2.12
1980	2.01	2.16	1.91	2.26		2.13	1.68	1.55	1.68	1.66	1.89	2.05
1981	2.02	2.10	1.88	2.22		2.06	1.63	1.54	1.71	1.57	1.94	2.04
1982		2.10	1.79	2.31			1.62	1.55	1.70	1.57	1.93	
1983		2.07							1.59			

[a] Sources: Compiled from Teitelbaum (1973, Table 1), except as indicated by footnotes. For 1971 to the latest available date, we have used unpublished tabulations of Institut Nationale d'Études Démographiques, GC/111, 19 March 1984.

[b] Data from 1920 to 1930 are for whites only.

[c] From 1957 to 1967, Soviet figures refer to years 1957–1958, 1958–1959, and so forth.

[d] Calot and Blayo (1982, p. 351).

[e] Pressat (1972, p. 823, Table 11).

[f] Festy (1979, p. 292).

[g] Blayo and Festy (1975, p. 884, Table 1).

[h] Ghetau (1978, p. 430, Table 3).

[i] Festy (1979, p. 274).

[j] Feshbach (1982, pp. 20–21).

[k] Festy (1974, p. 822, Table 4).

[l] Festy (1979, p. 297).

APPENDIX B: EUROPEAN ECONOMIC COMMUNITY RESOLUTION ON MEASURES TO PROMOTE POPULATION GROWTH (1984)*

The European Parliament,

(A) aware that Europe's standing and influence in the world depend largely on the vitality of its population and on the confidence placed by parents in the future and well-being of their children and the prospect of giving them a proper upbringing and education in a balanced family environment,

(B) seriously disturbed by the recent statistics showing a rapid decline in the total fertility rate in the EEC, which fell from 2.79 in 1964 to 1.68 in 1982 [translation corrected],

(C) whereas, unless steps are taken to reverse this trend, the population of the Europe of Ten will account for only 4.5 percent of the total world population by the year 2000 and only 2.3 percent by 2025, as opposed to 8.8 percent in 1950,

(D) having regard to the disappointing outcome of the informal meeting of the Ministers for Social Affairs and Employment in Paris on 5 April 1984,

1 Considers that population trends in Europe will have a decisive effect on the development of Europe and will determine the significance of the role which Europe will play in the world in future decades;

2 Considers that measures to combat this marked trend towards population decline, which is common to all the Member States, could usefully be taken at the Community level and would be of both political and social significance;

3 Calls on the Council of Social Affairs Ministers of the EEC to hold a further meeting to study the practical measures which could be taken, notably on the basis of suggestions by the President-in-Office, and calls on the Commission to submit proposals on this subject;

4 Instructs its President to forward this resolution to the Council and the Commission.

*Resolution No. C 127/78, 14.5.84. Reprinted with permission from the *Population and Development Review*, "The European Parliament on the Need for Promoting Population Growth" (September 1984), pp. 569–570.

APPENDIX C: U.S. POLICY STATEMENT AT THE UNITED NATIONS INTERNATIONAL CONFERENCE ON POPULATION (1984)*

Introduction

For many years, the United States has supported, and helped to finance, programs of family planning, particularly in developing countries. This Administration has continued that support but has placed it within a policy context different from that of the past. It is sufficiently evident that the current exponential growth in global population cannot continue indefinitely. There is no question of the ultimate need to achieve a condition of population equilibrium. The differences that do exist concern the choice of strategies and methods for the achievement of that goal. The experience of the last two decades not only makes possible but requires a sharper focus for our population policy. It requires a more refined approach to problems which appear today in quite a different light than they did twenty years ago.

First and most important, population growth is, of itself, a neutral phenomenon. It is not necessarily good or ill. It becomes an asset or a problem only in conjunction with other factors, such as economic policy, social constraints, need for manpower, and so forth. The relationship between population growth and economic development is not necessarily a negative one. More people do not necessarily mean less growth. Indeed, in the economic history of many nations, population growth has been an essential element in economic progress.

Before the advent of governmental population programs, several factors had combined to create an unprecedented surge in population over most of the world. Although population levels in many industrialized nations had reached or were approaching equilibrium in the period before the Second World War, the baby boom that followed in its wake resulted in a dramatic, but temporary, population "tilt" toward youth. The disproportionate number of infants, children, teenagers, and eventually young adults did strain the social infrastructure of schools, health facilities, law enforcement, and so forth. However, it also helped sustain strong eco-

*Held in Mexico City in August 1984.

nomic growth, despite occasionally counterproductive government policies.

Among the developing nations, a coincidental population increase was caused by entirely different factors. A tremendous expansion of health services—from simple inoculations to sophisticated surgery—saved millions of lives every year. Emergency relief, facilitated by modern transport, helped millions to survive flood, famine, and drought. The sharing of technology, the teaching of agriculture and engineering, and improvements in educational standards generally, all helped to reduce mortality rates, especially infant mortality, and to lengthen life spans.

This demonstrated not poor planning or bad policy but human progress in a new era of international assistance, technological advance, and human compassion. The population boom was a challenge; it need not have been a crisis. Seen in its broader context, it required a measured, modulated response. It provoked an overreaction by some, largely because it coincided with two negative factors which, together, hindered families and nations in adapting to their changing circumstances.

The first of these factors was governmental control of economies, a development which effectively constrained economic growth. The post-war experience consistently demonstrated that, as economic decision-making was concentrated in the hands of planners and public officials, the ability of average men and women to work towards a better future was impaired, and sometimes crippled. In many cases, agriculture was devastated by government price fixing that wiped out rewards for labor. Job creation in infant industries was hampered by confiscatory taxes. Personal industry and thrift were penalized, while dependence upon the state was encouraged. Political considerations made it difficult for an economy to adjust to changes in supply and demand or to disruptions in world trade and finance. Under such circumstances, population growth changed from an asset in the development of economic potential to a peril.

One of the consequences of this "economic statism" was that it disrupted the natural mechanism for slowing population growth in problem areas. The world's more affluent nations have reached a population equilibrium without compulsion and, in most cases, even before it was government policy to achieve it. The controlling factor in these cases has been the adjustment, by individual families, of reproductive behavior to economic opportunity and aspiration. Historically, as opportunities and the standard of living rise, the birth rate falls. In many countries, economic freedom has led to economically rational behavior.

That pattern might be well under way in many nations where population growth is today a problem, if counterproductive government policies had not disrupted economic incentives, rewards, and advancement. In this regard, localized crises of population growth are, in part, evidence of too much government control and planning, rather than too little.

The second factor that turned the population boom into a crisis was confined to the western world. It was an outbreak of an anti-intellectualism, which attacked science, technology, and the very concept of material progress. Joined to a commendable and long overdue concern for the environment, it was more a reflection of anxiety about unsettled times and an uncertain future. In its disregard of human experience and scientific sophistication, it was not unlike other waves of cultural anxiety that have swept through western civilization during times of social stress and scientific exploration.

The combination of these two factors—counterproductive economic policies in poor and struggling nations, and a pessimism among the more advanced—led to a demographic overreaction in the 1960s and 1970s. Scientific forecasts were required to compete with unsound, extremist scenarios, and too many governments pursued population control measures without sound economic policies that create the rise in living standards historically associated with decline in fertility rates. This approach has not worked, primarily because it has focused on a symptom and neglected the underlying ailments. For the last three years, this Administration has sought to reverse that approach. We recognize that, in some cases, immediate population pressures may require short-term efforts to ameliorate them. But population control programs alone cannot substitute for the economic reforms that put a society on the road toward growth and, as an aftereffect, toward slower population increase as well.

Nor can population control substitute for the rapid and responsible development of natural resources. In commenting on the

Global 2000 report, this Administration in 1981 disagreed with its call ''for more governmental supervision and control,'' stating that:

> Historically, that has lended to restrict the availability of resources and to hamper the development of technology, rather than to assist it. Recognizing the seriousness of environmental and economic problems, and their relationship to social and political pressures, especially in the developing nations, the Administration places a priority upon technological advance and economic expansion, which hold out the hope of prosperity and stability of a rapidly changing world. That hope can be realized, of course, only to the extent that government's response to problems, whether economic or ecological, respects and enhances individual freedom, which makes true progress possible and worthwhile.

Those principles underlie this country's approach to the International Conference on Population to be held in Mexico City in August.

Policy Objectives

The world's rapid population growth is a recent phenomenon. Only several decades ago, the population of developing countries was relatively stable, the result of a balance between high fertility and high mortality. There are now 4.5 billion people in the world, and six billion are projected by the year 2000. Such rapid growth places tremendous pressures on governments without concomitant economic growth.

The International Conference on Population offers the US an opportunity to strengthen the international consensus on the interrelationships between economic development and population which has emerged since the last such conference in Bucharest in 1974. Our primary objective will be to encourage developing countries to adopt sound economic policies and, where appropriate, population policies consistent with respect for human dignity and family values. As President Reagan stated in his message to the Mexico City Conference:

> We believe population programs can and must be truly voluntary, cognizant of the rights and responsibilities of individuals and families, and respectful of religious and cultural values. When they are, such programs can make an important contribution to economic and social development,

to the health of mothers and children, and to the stability of the family and of society.

US support for family planning programs is based on respect for human life, enhancement of human dignity, and strengthening of the family. Attempts to use abortion, involuntary sterilization, or other coercive measures in family planning must be shunned, whether exercised against families within a society or against nations within the family of man.

The United Nations Declaration of the Rights of the Child [1959] calls for legal protection for children before birth as well as after birth. In keeping with this obligation, the United States does not consider abortion an acceptable element of family planning programs and will no longer contribute to those of which it is a part. Accordingly, when dealing with nations which support abortion with funds not provided by the United States Government, the United States will contribute to such nations through segregated accounts which cannot be used for abortion. Moreover, the United States will no longer contribute to separate nongovernmental organizations which perform or actively promote abortion as a method of family planning in other nations. With regard to the United Nations Fund for Population Activities [UNFPA], the US will insist that no part of its contribution be used for abortion. The US will also call for concrete assurances that the UNFPA is not engaged in, or does not provide funding for, abortion or coercive family planning programs; if such assurances are not forthcoming, the US will redirect the amount of its contribution to other, non-UNFPA, family planning programs.

In addition, when efforts to lower population growth are deemed advisable, US policy considers it imperative that such efforts respect the religious beliefs and culture of each society, and the right of couples to determine the size of their own families. Accordingly, the US will not provide family planning funds to any nation which engages in forcible coercion to achieve population growth objectives.

US Government authorities will immediately begin negotiations to implement the above policies with the appropriate governments and organizations.

It is time to put additional emphasis upon those root problems, which frequently exacerbate population pressures, but which have too often been given scant attention. By focusing upon real remedies for underdeveloped economies, the International Conference on Population can reduce demographic issues to their proper place. It is an important place, but not the controlling one. It requires our continuing attention within the broader context of economic growth and of the economic freedom that is its prerequisite.

Population, Development, and Economic Policies

Conservative projections indicate that, in the sixty years from 1950 to 2010, many Third World countries will experience four, five, or even sixfold increases in the size of their populations. Even under the assumption of gradual declines in birth rates, the unusually high proportion of youth in the Third World means that the annual population growth in many of these countries will continue to increase for the next several decades.

Sound economic policies and a market economy are of fundamental importance to the process of economic development. Rising standards of living contributed in a major way to the demographic transition from high to low rates of population growth which occurred in the US and other industrialized countries over the last century.

The current situation of many developing countries, however, differs in certain ways from conditions in 19th century Europe and the US. The rates and dimensions of population growth are much higher now, the pressures on land, water, and resources are greater, the safety-valve of migration is more restricted, and, perhaps most important, time is not on their side because of the momentum of demographic change.

Rapid population growth compounds already serious problems faced by both public and private sectors in accommodating changing social and economic demands. It diverts resources from needed investment, and increases the costs and difficulties of economic development. Slowing population growth is not a panacea for the problems of social and economic development. It is not offered as a substitute for sound and comprehensive development policies which encourage a vital private sector; it cannot solve problems of hunger, unemployment, crowding, or social disorder.

Population assistance is an ingredient of a comprehensive program that focuses on the root causes of development failures. The US program as a whole, including population assistance, lays the basis for well-grounded, step-by-step initiatives to improve the well-being of people in developing countries and to make their own efforts, particularly through expanded private sector initiatives, a key building block of development programs.

Fortunately, a broad international consensus has emerged since the 1974 Bucharest World Population Conference that economic development and population policies are mutually reinforcing.

By helping developing countries slow their population growth through support for effective voluntary family planning programs, in conjunction with sound economic policies, US population assistance contributes to stronger saving and investment rates, speeds the development of effective markets and related employment opportunities, reduces the potential resource requirements of programs to improve the health and education of the people, and hastens the achievement of each country's graduation from the need for external assistance.

The United States will continue its longstanding commitment to development assistance, of which population programs are a part. We recognize the importance of providing our assistance within the cultural, economic, and political context of the countries we are assisting, and in keeping with our own values.

Health and Humanitarian Concerns

Perhaps the most poignant consequence of rapid population growth is its effect on the health of mothers and children. Especially in poor countries, the health and nutrition status of women and children is linked to family size. Maternal and infant mortality rises with the number of births and with births too closely spaced. In countries as different as Turkey, Peru, and Nepal, a child born less than two years after its sibling is twice as likely to die before it reaches the age of five, than if there were an interval of at least four years between the births. Complications of pregnancy are

169

more frequent among women who are very young or near the end of their reproductive years. In societies with widespread malnutrition and inadequate health conditions, these problems are reinforced; numerous and closely spaced births lead to even greater malnutrition of mothers and infants.

It is an unfortunate reality that, in many countries, abortion is used as a means of terminating unwanted pregnancies. This is unnecessary and repugnant; voluntary family assistance programs can provide a humane alternative to abortion for couples who wish to regulate the size of their family, and evidence from some developing countries indicates a decline in abortion as such services become available.

The basic objective of all US assistance, including population programs, is the betterment of the human condition—improving the quality of life of mothers and children, of families, and of communities for generations to come. For we recognize that people are the ultimate resource—but this means happy and healthy children, growing up with education, finding productive work as young adults, and able to develop their full mental and physical potential.

US aid is designed to promote economic progress in developing countries through encouraging sound economic policies and freeing of individual initiative. Thus, the US supports a broad range of activities in various sectors, including agriculture, private enterprise, science and technology, health, population, and education. Population assistance amounts to about ten percent of total development assistance.

Technology as a Key to Development

The transfer, adaptation, and improvement of modern know-how is central to US development assistance. People with greater know-how are people better able to improve their lives. Population assistance ensures that a wide range of modern demographic technology is made available to developing countries and that technological improvements critical for successful development receive support.

The efficient collection, processing, and analysis of data derived from census, survey, and vital statistics programs contribute to better planning in both the public and private sectors.

APPENDIX D: RESOLUTION BY RUMANIAN COMMUNIST
PARTY ON POPULATION POLICY (1984)*

In accordance with the provisions of the Party's Program for the establishment of a broadly developed socialist society and the advancement of Romania toward communism, and with the tasks and directives laid down by Comrade Nicolae Ceauşescu, General Secretary of the Romanian Communist Party and President of the Socialist Republic of Romania, an increase in the birth rate, efforts to ensure adequate population growth, and the strengthening of the family must constitute priority objectives for the development of our socialist nation in order to ensure the economic and social progress of the country and preserve the vigor and youth of the entire people.

On the basis of general economic and social development, all the necessary conditions have been guaranteed in our socialist society for a general improvement in the people's state of health, for an increase in the birth rate, and for a natural population growth. An extensive network of health facilities has been set up, substantial funds have been allocated and are being allocated for crèches and kindergartens, for State allowances for children, and for grants and other types of support for large families. These have resulted in an improvement in the people's health and constitute—together with the other socioeconomic measures taken by the Party and the State—an important factor in the improvement of the quality of life in our country.

Analyzing the situation in this important area of our social life, the Executive Political Committee of the Central Committee of the Romanian Communist Party has noted that, although significant progress has been made in general health policy, there are still some serious shortcomings in the implementation of our Party's and State's demographic policy. For example, in the activities of the people's councils, of the Ministry of Health, and of the county boards of health and the Board of Health of the City of Bucharest, serious deficiencies are apparent as regards the implementation of

*Resolution made by the Executive Political Committee of the Central Committee of the Rumanian Communist Party on 3 March 1984. Reprinted with permission from the *Population and Development Review*, "Romanian Population Policy," Margaret Roberts (trans.), 10, 3 (September 1984), pp. 570–573.

the policy of our Party and State in the area of strengthening the family and increasing the birth rate. It must also be pointed out that neither the county party committees nor the other party organs and organizations have acted as they should in this respect; they have not exercised careful and continuing supervision over the activities performed by the health organs in matters relating to growth of the birth index and other demographic phenomena.

In its discussion of the Report on population trends and trends in the major demographic phenomena in 1983, the Executive Political Committee of the Central Committee of the Romanian Communist Party noted that the birth rate in 1983 was 14.3 live births per thousand inhabitants as against 19.7 in 1975.

Analyzing this situation, the Executive Political Committee and the General Secretary of the Party, Comrade Nicolae Ceauşescu, considered that it was due primarily to insufficient firmness and a lack of concern on the part of the Ministry of Health, the health organs, the party, mass and public organs and organizations, and the people's councils in combatting and curbing abusive and unwarranted practices regarding the termination of pregnancies. Last year the number of terminated pregnancies increased to 421,386, while the number of births was 321,498, so that there was a ratio of 1,311 terminated pregnancies for each 1,000 live births.

In view of this intolerable situation the Ministry of Health and the health authorities were sharply criticized for not taking timely and decisive measures to establish order in this area and to completely eliminate all unnecessary terminations of pregnancy, as some physicians have been using this expedient to create lucrative sources of profit for themselves at the expense of the population. It was noted that the practice of terminating pregnancies is an antinational and antisocial action, as it prevents the normal development of our people, and the most resolute action—in keeping with the laws and regulations—was demanded to combat and eliminate it.

The General Secretary of the Party and President of the Socialist Republic of Romania, Comrade Nicolae Ceauşescu, in his noble and constant concern for the future of our socialist nation and for the implementation of the Party's Program to increase the general well-being of the people, has prescribed a set of measures designed to increase the birth rate to 19–20 per thousand population per year.

In the spirit of these directives and guidelines the Executive Political Committee of the Central Committee of the Romanian Communist Party hereby decides that:

(1) The county party committees and the other party organs and organizations shall organize thorough studies and discussions on demographic trends and prescribe, in the light of the particular situation in each county, specific measures and tasks for all responsible elements in this field.

(2) The activities of the party organs and organizations, of the people's councils, and of the other central and local bodies must focus on the priority objective of ensuring an adequate natural growth in the population and solving problems relating to the growth of the birth rate and the strengthening of the family. The utmost order and discipline must be established in the enforcement of existing laws and regulations prohibiting terminations of pregnancy. The county committees, together with all responsible elements in this field, must undertake a monthly analysis of demographic developments in their respective counties and must prescribe, on that basis, specific measures for the decisive removal of the factors preventing an adequate increase in the rate of natural increase of the population.

Under the leadership of the county party committees, the county people's councils shall organize, with the support of the Ministry of Health, periodic debates on demographic phenomena in their respective territories and—on the basis of the legislative provisions and the programs in force—shall prescribe measures for a more decisive involvement and increased responsibility on the part of all elements having obligations in connection with the performance of the tasks of strengthening the family and increasing the birth rate.

(3) The party organs and organizations shall strengthen control over the manner in which the health units promote the health of women, and improvements in the supervision of pregnant women, medical care during childbirth, and the normal development of infants and children. In counties in which unsatisfactory demographic indicators are recorded, the Ministry of Health, together with the county people's councils and the People's Council of the City of Bucharest, shall organize comprehensive control mechanisms for the detection and study of the causes of these phenomena, and take the necessary measures.

(4) The county party organs, the people's councils, the Ministry

of Health, the county boards of health, and the Board of Health of the City of Bucharest shall exercise continuing surveillance, through their own machinery and through specialized groups, over the manner in which the laws and regulations in force concerning termination of the normal course of pregnancies are observed in maternity hospitals and in specialists' offices, they shall take every care to prohibit termination of the normal course of a pregnancy and shall intervene forcefully to ensure strict application of the law in all cases where the rules are found to be violated or disregarded.

Furthermore, the Ministry of Health and the boards of health, together with the organs of State, shall be required to intensify the organization of systematic control mechanisms in all counties, and particularly in those where a large number of pregnancy terminations have been reported, to take the necessary measures to put a complete end to inadmissable practices in this field. Severe measures, in accordance with the provisions of the law, shall be taken against medical cadres and health personnel involved in the performance of illegal pregnancy terminations. The Ministry of Health, the county boards of health, the central disciplinary board, and the county disciplinary boards for health personnel shall refer to the collectives concerned all cases of medical cadres guilty of unwarranted pregnancy terminations and shall prescribe firm measures to prevent any abuses and illegalities of this kind.

(5) The Ministry of Health, as the specialized State organ in the field of public health and the organ that bears full responsibility for the strict application and observance of the country's laws concerning normal and adequate population growth, must be more exacting and exercise strict control to ensure exemplary performance by all elements of the tasks assigned to them in the matter of implementing the country's demographic policy.

(6) While promoting and strongly supporting an increase in the birth rate, the people's councils, the Ministry of Health, the county boards of health, and the Board of Health of the City of Bucharest shall take all necessary measures to improve the activities of the maternal and child health units within the medical-health system and to increase the responsibility of all cadres with a view to the further reduction of infant mortality. To that end the Ministry of Health shall arrange for the transfer to the counties of specialized cadres from the research institutes and university clinics, so as to improve the quality of medical care for the mother and child.

(7) The county, city, town, and communal committees and the other party, mass, and public organs and organizations shall intensify their work of patriotic, moral and civic, and health education and shall extensively debate, in each unit, the problems connected with promoting marriages, strengthening the family, and increasing the latter's role in the development of society.

(8) The Union of Communist Youth, the National Women's Council, the General Trade Union Confederation, and the Red Cross Society shall organize, at the city, town, and communal levels, in the socialist units, with the support of the party organs and organizations, broad action to publicize and popularize the measures taken by our socialist State to protect the mother and child, to strengthen the role of the family as the basic nucleus of society, and to encourage among youth and other working people a healthy attitude toward marriage, the family, and society.

(9) The central and local press, and the radio and television service shall organize—with support from the Ministry of Health—special broadcasts and features and extensive debates on the problems relating to, and measures required for, a growth in the birth rate and for ensuring natural population growth, the development of the family, and the care and education of the child.

(10) The National Demographic Commission, which is responsible for monitoring implementation of the measures laid down by the Party and State leadership regarding population trends, shall periodically analyze demographic indicators and propose measures to improve activities in this field.

(11) The Supreme Health Council shall periodically analyze demographic developments in our country and, on that basis, prescribe specific measures and tasks for the further improvement of activities in the medical and health field, to ensure the health of the population and the rise in the birth rate.

The Executive Political Committee expresses its conviction that the party organs and organizations, the mass and public organizations, the Ministry of Health, and the other central organs will take decisive and responsible action to implement party and State policy in matters relating to demography and increased natural population growth, thus contributing to the general development of our nation and to a steady rise in its level of civilization and well-being.

The Executive Political Committee of the Central Committee of the Romanian Communist Party appeals, at this time, to the entire population and to the working people of the towns and villages, to understand that the task of ensuring normal demographic growth in the population is a high honor and a patriotic duty for every family and for all our people, who have always taken pride in strong families, with many children, whom they have raised with love, thus ensuring the vitality, youth, and vigor of the entire nation. Today, more than ever before, we have the important duty to ensure for our country successive new generations that will contribute to the prosperity of our socialist nation and to the triumph of socialism and communism in Romania.

APPENDIX E: THE HEIDELBERG MANIFESTO (1982)*

It is with grave concern that we observe the infiltration of the German nation by millionfold waves of foreigners and their families, the infiltration of our language, our culture, and our national characteristics by foreign influences. In 1980 alone, despite the freeze on hiring, the number of registered foreigners increased by 309,000, including 194,000 Turks. Our birth rate is now barely one-half the rate needed to ensure the continued existence of our nation. Many Germans are already strangers in the places where they live and work.

The immigration of foreigners was encouraged by the Federal Government for reasons connected with uncontrolled economic growth, which is now seen as a dubious phenomenon. The German people were given no explanations regarding the significance and the consequences of this policy, and they were also not consulted on it. For this reason we call for the establishment of an association that, independent of parties and ideologies, will work for the preservation of the German people and its spiritual identity on the basis of our Western, Christian heritage. On the basis of the

*This document was prepared by 15 prominent West German university professors and scholars from a variety of disciplines, calling themselves the "Heidelberg circle." It originally appeared in the 5 February 1982 edition of the newspaper *Die Zeit*. Reprinted with permission from the *Population and Development Review*, "The Heidelberg Manifesto: A German Reaction to Immigration," Eileen B. Hennessy (trans.), 8, 3 (September 1982), pp. 636–637.

Constitution we reject ideological nationalism, racism, and the extremism of the Right and the Left.

Biologically and cybernetically, nations are living systems of a higher order, with different system qualities that are transmitted genetically and by tradition. The integration of large masses of non-German foreigners and the preservation of our nation thus cannot be achieved simultaneously; it will lead to the well-known ethnic catastrophes of multicultural societies.

Every people, including the German people, has a natural right to preserve its identity and its individuality in its habitat. Respect for other peoples requires their preservation but not their fusion ("Germanization"). We regard Europe as an organism of peoples and nations that are worthy of preservation on the basis of their common history. "Every nation is a unique facet of a Divine Plan" (Solzhenitsyn).

The Constitution of the Federal Republic of Germany does not posit the concept of "the nation" as the sum total of all the peoples within a state. It is based on the concept of "a people," specifically the German people. The President of the Republic and the Members of Parliament take an oath of office to dedicate their strength "to the well-being of the German people, to promote its advantage, and to defend it from harm." The Constitution thus makes the preservation of the German people an obligation.

In the Preamble to the Constitution, the goal of reunification is established as an obligation. How is this obligation to be met if a portion of the nation's territory becomes ethnically foreign? The current policy toward foreigners promotes the development of a multi-racial society. This is in violation of the Constitution, which obligates all Germans of the Federal Republic to protect and defend our people's right to exist.

Hundreds of thousands of children are now illiterate in their native languages and in German. What hope for the future can they have? And our own children, who are being educated in classrooms where the majority of students are foreigners: what hope for the future can they have? Will the billions being spent for the defense of our country ultimately be worth such a price?

Only vigorous and intact German families can preserve our people for the future. Our own children are the only foundation for the future of Germany and Europe.

Tehnological development offers, and will increasingly offer, opportunities to make all employment of foreigners unnecessary. Bringing the machine to the human being, rather than the human being to the machine, must therefore be the highest guiding principle for the economy.

The problem must be attacked at its roots, and this means concerted development assistance to improve the living conditions of the foreign workers in their native countries—not here in our country. For the Federal Republic of Germany, which is one of the most heavily populated countries of the world, the return of the foreigners to their native lands will provide ecological as well as social relief.

To achieve continued public response, we call upon all organizations, associations, citizens' groups, and other groups to dedicate themselves to the preservation of our people, our language, our culture, and our way of life, and to form an umbrella organization that will permit both group and individual membership, with each association retaining complete independence and freedom. A supervisory board should be appointed to oversee the work of this organization and to protect its ideological and political independence.

References

Abel, R. *The Pragmatic Humanism of F. C. S. Schiller*. New York: Columbia Univ. Press, 1955.

Baguley, D. *Fécondité d'Émile Zola*. Toronto: Toronto Univ. Press, 1978.

Balck, J. A. "Recruiting in the German Army." *Journal of the Royal Army Medical Corps* 15 (1910).

Banks, J. A. *Prosperity and Parenthood*. London: Routledge & Kegan Paul, 1954.

Bazin, R. *La terre qui meurt*. Paris: C. Lévy, 1899.

Beale, O. C. *Racial Decay: A Compilation of Evidence from World Sources*. London: A. C. Fifield, 1911.

Bean, F. "The baby boom and its explanations." *Sociological Abstracts* 24 (Summer 1983).

Becker, G. S. "An economic analysis of fertility." In National Bureau of Economic Research, *Demographic and Economic Change in Developed Countries*, Princeton: Princeton Univ. Press, 1960.

Besemeres, J. F. *Socialist Population Politics*. White Plains, N.Y.: M. E. Sharpe, 1980.

Blacker, C. P. *Birth Control and the State*. London: Kegan Paul & Co., 1926.

Blacker, C. P. *Voluntary Sterilization*. London: Oxford Univ. Press, 1934.

Blayo, C., and Festy, P. "La fécondité à l'est et à l'ouest de l'Europe." *Population* 29 (July–Oct. 1975).

Boston Women's Health Book Collective. *Our Bodies, Our Selves*. New York: Simon & Schuster, 1976.

Bourget, P. *L'Étape*. Paris: plon-Nourrit, 1902.

Bouthoul, G. *La population dans le monde*. Paris: Payot, 1935.

Bouvier, L. F., and Davis, C. E. *The Future Racial Composition of the United States*. Washington, D.C., U.S. Government Printing Office, 1982.

Bowman, E. M. *The Early Novels of Paul Bourget*. New York: Columbia Univ. Press, 1925.

Brieux, E. *Les trois filles de M. Dupont*. Paris: P.-V. Stock, 1899.

British Association. *Report of the Papers and Discussion at the Cambridge Meeting of the British Association, 1904, on the Alleged Physical Deterioration of the People and the Utility of an Anthropometric Survey*. London: Anthropological Institute of Great Britain and Ireland, 1905.

British Parliamentary Papers. *Royal Commission on Physical Training in Scotland, 1903*, vol. xxx, Cd 5107, 5108.

179

REFERENCES

British Parliamentary Papers. *Interdepartmental Committee on Physical Deterioration*, 1904, vol. 32, Cd 2175, 2186, 2210.

British Parliamentary Papers. *Report on Social Insurance and Allied Services*, 1942, vol. 30, Cmd 6404.

Burns, C. M. *Infant and Maternal Mortality in Relation to Size of Family and Rapidity of Breeding*. Newcastle-upon-Tyne: King's College, Univ. of Durham, Department of Physiology, 1942.

Burns, E. "Émile Zola: pages d'exil." *Nottingham French Studies* 3 (1964).

Calot, G., and Blayo, C. "The recent course of fertility in Western Europe." *Population Studies* 36, 3 (Nov. 1982).

Calot, G., and Hecht, J. "The control of fertility trends." In Council of Europe, *Population Decline in Europe*. (London: Edward Arnold, 1978).

Canada. *Demographic Aspects of Immigration*. Report of a meeting, 14 December 1984, Montreal, 1984a.

Canada. *Labor Market Aspects of Immigration*. Report of a meeting, 4 December 1984, Toronto, 1984b.

Canada. *Social and Humanitarian Aspects of Immigration*. Report of a meeting, 30 November 1984, Hull, 1984c.

Chambre, H. "L'Evolution de la legislation familiale soviètique de 1917 à 1952." In R. Priagent, (ed.), *Renouveau des idées sur la famille*. Paris: Institut National d'Études Démographiques, 1954.

Charles, E. *The Menace of Under-population: A Biological Study of the Decline of Population Growth*. London: Watts & Co., 1936.

Chaunu, P. *La réfus de la vie*. Paris: Calmann-Lévy, 1975.

Chevalier, L. *The Labouring Classes and the Dangerous Classes of Nineteenth Century Paris*. London: Routledge & Kegan Paul, 1966.

Chirac, J. "Jacques Chirac on French population issues." *Population and Development Review* 11 (1985).

Coale, A. J. "How the age distribution of a human population is determined." *Cold Spring Harbor Symposia on Quantitative Biology* 22 (1957).

Coale, A. J. "The demographic transition reconsidered." In *Proceedings of the IUSSP International Population Congress, 1973*.

Coale, A. J. Anderson, B., and Härm, E. *Human Fertility in Russia since the Nineteenth Century*. Princeton: Princeton Univ. Press, 1979.

Council of Europe. *Population Decline in Europe*. London: Edward Arnold, 1978.

Council of Europe. *Recent Demographic Developments in the Member States of the Council of Europe*. Strasbourg: Council of Europe, 1982.

Cowan, R. S. "Francis Galton's contribution to genetics." *Journal of the History of Biology* 5 (1972).

Crackanthorpe, M. "Population and progress." *Fortnightly Review* 86 (1906).

Darwin, L. "The racial effects of public assistance." *Charity Organisation Review* 267 (1917).

Darwin, L. *The Need for Eugenic Reform*. London: John Murray, 1926.

Darwin, L. *What Is Eugenics?* London: Watts & Co., 1928.

David, H. P., and McIntyre, R. J. *Reproductive Behavior: Central and Eastern European Experience*. New York: Springer Publishing Company, 1981.

Davis, C., and Feshbach, M. "Rising infant mortality in the USSR in the 1970s." U.S. Bureau of the Census, *International Population Reports*, ser. F-95, no. 74. Washington, D.C.: U.S. Government Printing Office, 1980.

Debré, R., and Sauvy, A. *Des Français pour la France: La problème de la population.* Paris, Gallinard, 1946.

Desfosses, H. (ed.), *Soviet Population Policy: Conflicts and Constraints.* New York: Pergamon, 1981.

DiMaio, A. J. "Evolution of Soviet population thought: From Marxism-Leninism to the *Literaturnaya Gazeta* debate." In H. Desfosses (ed.), *Soviet Population Policy: Conflicts and Constraints.* New York: Pergamon, 1981.

Dumont, A. *Dépopulation et civilisation: Étude démographique.* Paris: Lecrosnier et Babé, 1890.

Dumont, G. F., *La France ridée: Échapper à la logique du déclin.* Paris: Librairie generale française, 1979.

East, E. M. "Population." *Scientific Monthly* 10 (1920).

Easterlin, R. A. "The conflict between aspirations and resources." *Population and Development Review* 2 (1976).

Easterlin, R. A. *Birth and Fortune.* New York: Basic Books, 1980.

Ehrlich, P. *The Population Bomb.* New York: Riverside Press, 1968.

Ermisch, J. "Investigations into the causes of the postwar fertility swings." In D. Eversley and W. Köllmann (eds.), *Population Change and Social Planning.* London: Edward Arnold, 1982.

Ermisch, J. *The Political Economy of Demographic Change.* London: Heinemann, 1983.

Eugenics and the State. Baltimore: Williams & Wilkins, 1923.

Eugenics, Genetics and the Family. Baltimore: Williams & Wilkins, 1923.

Eugenics in Race and State. Baltimore: Williams &Wilkins, 1923.

Eversley, D., and Köllmann, W. (eds.), *Population Change and Social Planning.* London, Edward Arnold, 1982.

Ferenczi, D. "La politique économique mondiale et les changements dans la population." *Revue économique internationale* 2 (1934).

Feshbach, M. "The Soviet Union: Population trends and dilemmas." *Population Bulletin* 37, 3 (1982).

Festy, P. "La situation démographique des deux Allemagnes." *Population* 28 (July–Oct. 1974).

Festy, P. *La fécondité des pays occidentaux de 1870 à 1970.* Paris: Institut National d'Études Démographiques, 1979.

Fischer, E. "Report on Meckermann's studies of the differential fertility within certain social groups in Germany." In G. Pitt-Rivers (ed.), *Problems of Population.* London: G. Allen & Unwin, 1932.

Fisher, R. A. *The Genetical Theory of Natural Selection.* Oxford: Clarendon Press, 1930.

Ford, K. "Contraceptive use in the United States, 1973–1976." *Family Planning Perspectives* 10, 5 (Sept.–Oct. 1978).

Forrest, D. W. *Francis Galton: The Life and Work of a Victorian Genius.* London: Elek, 1974.

Foville, A. de. "Enquête sur le dépeuplement de la France." *La Revue Hebdomadaire* 5 (1909).

REFERENCES

Freeden, M. "Eugenics and progressive thought: A study in ideological affinity." *Historical Journal* 22 (1979).

Frejka, T. "Family assistance in Europe: Social welfare measures or pronatalist policies?" *People* (London) 3 (1982).

Gadille, J. *La pensée et l'action politique des évêques français au débût de la IIIè république*. Paris: Hachette, 1967.

Galton, F. *Hereditary Genius*. London: Macmillan & Co., 1869.

Galton, F. *Memories of My Life*. London: Methuen & Co., 1908.

Gambrell, R. D., Jr., Maier, R. C., and Sanders, B. I. "Decreased incidence of breast cancer in postmenapausal oestrogen-progestogen users." *Obstetrics and Gynacology* 62 (1983).

Gates, R. Ruggles. "Eugenics and education." *Eugenics Review* 23 (1932a).

Gates, R. Ruggles. "Notes of the quarter." *Eugenics Review* 23 (1932b).

Ghetau, V. "L'évolution de la fécondité en Roumanie." *Population* 32 (March–April 1978).

Gilbert, B. B. *The Evolution of National Insurance in Great Britain*. London: Michael Joseph, 1966.

Gini, C. "The war from the eugenic point of view." In *Eugenics and the State*. Baltimore: Williams & Wilkins, 1923.

Grass, G. *Headbirths, or the Germans Are Dying Out*, R. Manheim (trans.) New York and London: Harcourt Brace Jovanovich, 1982.

Guedella, P. *The Two Marshalls: Bazaine and Pétain*. London: Hodder & Stoughton, 1943.

Guiral, P. "Vue d'ensemble sur l'idée de race et la gauche française." In P. Guiral and E. Temime (eds.), *L'Idée de race dans la pensée politique française contemporaine*. Paris: CNRS, 1977.

Haldane, J. B. S. *Heredity an Politics*. London: G. Allen & Unwin, 1938.

Haller, M. *Eugenics: Hereditarian Attitudes in American Thought*. New Brunswick, N.J.: Rutgers Univ. Press, 1963.

Harris, J. *William Beveridge: A Biography*. Oxford: Oxford Univ. Press, 1977.

Hemmings, F. W. J. *The Life and Times of Émile Zola*. London: Elck, 1977.

Henshaw, S. K., and O'Reilly, K. "Characteristics of abortion patients in the United States, 1979 and 1980." *Family Planning Perspectives* 11, 1 (Jan.–Feb. 1983).

Heron, D. *On the Relation of Fertility in Man to Social Status, and on the Changes in the Relations That Have Taken Place during the Last Fifty Years*. London: University College, London, 1906.

Hewitt, M. *Wives and Mothers in Victorian Industry*. London: Rockliff, 1958.

Hobson, J. A. *Imperialism*. London: James Nisbet, 1902.

Hogben, L. *Genetic Principles in Medicine and Social Science*. London: Williams & Norgate, 1931.

Hogben, L. "Heredity and human affairs." In J. A. Thomson (ed.), *Science Today*. London: Eyre & Spottiswoode, 1934.

Hogben, L. *The Retreat from Reason*. London: Watts & Co., 1936.

Hunter, J. C. "The problem of the French birth rate on the eve of World War I." *French Historical Studies* 2 (1962).

Huss, M.-M. *Demography, Public Opinion and Politics in France, 1974–1980*. Department of Geography, Queen Mary College, London, Occasional Paper No. 16 (1980).

Huxley, J. S. *Biology and Human Life*. London: British Science Guild, 1921.

Huxley, L. *Progress and the Unfit* London: Watts & Co., 1926.

Jobert, M. "Comment un pays meurt." In G. F. Dumont (ed.), *La France ridée: Échapper à la logique du declin*. Paris: 1979.

Jones, G. Stedman. *Outcast London*. Oxford: Oxford Univ. Press, 1971.

Journal Officiel: Débats du Chambre, 1937–1939.

Journal Officiel: Débats du Sénat, 1919.

Journal of Tropical Medicine and Hygiene. "War and population," 20 (1917).

Kalvemark, A.-S. *More Children or Better Quality? Aspects of Swedish Population Policy in the 1930s*. Stockholm: Almquist & Wiksell International, 1980.

Kamerman, S. B., and Kahn, A. J. *Child Care, Family Benefits, and Working Parents: A Study in Comparative Policy*. New York: Columbia Univ. Press, 1981.

Keyfitz, N. "Population theory and doctrine: A historical survey." In W. Peterson (ed.), *Readings in Population*. New York: Macmillan, 1972.

Keynes, J. M. "The economic consequences of a declining population." *Eugenics Review* 29 (1937).

Knodel, J. "Fertility trends in the United States, 1945–60." Ph.D. diss. Princeton, Princeton, N.J., 1968.

Knodel, J. *The Decline of Fertility in Germany, 1871–1939*. Princeton, N.J.: Princeton Univ. Press, 1974.

Kuczynski, R. *"Living Space" and Population Problems*. Oxford, Clarendon Press, 1939.

Lapouge, G. Vacher de. *L'Aryen: Son rôle sociale*. Paris: A. Fontemoing, 1899.

Lapouge, G. Vacher de. "La race chez les populations mélanges." In *Eugenics in Race and State*. Baltimore: Williams & Wilkins, 1923.

Le Fort, L. "Du mouvement de la population en France." *Revue des Deux Mondes* 69 (1869).

Lenin, V. I. *Imperialism*. Moscow: Foreign Languages Publishing House, 1947.

Leroy-Beaulieu, P. "La politique continentale et la politique coloniale." *L'economiste français* (7 May 1881).

Lesthaeghe, R. J. *The Decline of Belgian Fertility, 1800–1970*. Princeton, N.J.: Princeton Univ. Press, 1977.

Leybourne, G., and White, K. *Education and the Birth Rate*. London: Jonathan Cape, 1940.

Livi Bacci, M. *A Century of Portuguese Fertility*. Princeton, N.J.: Princeton Univ. Press, 1971.

Livi Bacci, M. *A History of Italian Fertility*. Princeton, N.J.: Princeton Univ. Press, 1977.

McCleary, G. F. *Infant Mortality and Infant Milk Depots*. London: P. S. King & Son, 1905.

McIntosh, C. A. *Population Policy in Western Europe: Responses to Low Fertility in France, Sweden and West Germany*. New York: M. E. Sharpe, 1983.

March, L. "The consequences of war on the birth rate in France." In *Eugenics, Genetics and the Family*. Baltimore: Williams & Wilkins, 1923.

Marchant, J. *Cradles or Coffins?* London: National Life Series, 1917.

REFERENCES

Marchant, J. (ed.). *The Control of Parenthood*. London: G. P. Putnam's Sons, 1920a.

Marchant, J. (ed.). *Problems of Population and Parenthood*. London: Chapman & Hall, 1920b.

Martial, R. *Race, heredité, folie*. Paris: Mereure de France, 1938.

Martial, R. *Vie et constance des races*. Paris: Mereure de France, 1939.

Martin, P. L., and Sehgal, E. B. "Illegal immigration: The guestworker option." *Public Policy* 28, 2 (1980).

Miller, M. J., and Martin, P. L. *Administering Foreign-Worker Programs: Lessons from Europe*. Lexington, Mass.: Lexington Books, 1982.

Mitchell, B. R. *European Historical Statistics, 1750–1975*. London: Macmillan, 1980.

Money, L. Chiozza. *The Peril of the White Race*. London: W. Collins Sons, 1925.

Monier, A. "L'Europe et les pays dévellopé d'outre mer: données statistiques." *Population* 35 (July–Oct. 1981).

Monod, H. *La santé publique*. Paris: Hachette, 1904.

Mosse, G. *Toward the Final Solution*. London: Dent, 1978.

Muller, H. J. *Out of the Night: A Biologist's View of the Future*. London: Victor Gollancz, 1936.

National Bureau of Economic Research, *Demographic and Economic Change in Developed Countries*. Princeton: 1960.

National Center for Health Statistics. "Advance report of final natality statistics, 1980." *Monthly Vital Statistics Report* 31, 8 (Supp.), (Nov. 30, 1982).

Newsholme, A. *The Declining Birth Rate: Its National and International Significance*. London: Cassell, 1906.

New York Times. "Soviets affirm rise in infant mortality," 21 June 1981.

Nitti, F. S. *Population and the Social System*. London: Sonnenschein, 1894.

Notestein, F. "Demography in the United States: A partial account of the development of the field." *Population and Development Review* 8 (1982).

Osborn, H. F. "Opening remarks." In *Eugenics, Genetics, and the Family*. Baltimore: Williams & Wilkins, 1923.

Paddock, W., and Paddock, P. *Famine, 1975!* London: Weidenfeld & Nicolson, 1968.

Petersen, W. "John Maynard Keynes's theories of population and the concept of 'optimum'." *Population Studies* 8 (1955).

Phelps, E. B. "The world-wide effort to diimish infant mortality—its present status and its possibilities." *Transactions of the Fifteenth International Congress on Hygiene and Demography* 6 (Washington, 1913).

Pike, M. C., Krailo, M. D., Henderson, B. E., Duke, A., and Roy, S. "Breast cancer in young women and use of oral contraceptives: Possible modifying effect of formulation and age at use." *Lancet* 2 (1983).

Piotrow, P. T. *World Population Crisis: The U.S. Response*. New York: Praeger, 1973.

Pollock, C. E. "Comparison of recruiting statistics in Germany and France for the year 1906." *Journal of the Royal Army Medical Corps* 14 (1910).

Population and Development Review. "The Heidelberg manifesto: A German reaction to immigration," 8 (1982).

Population and Development Review. "The European Parliament on the need for promoting population growth," 10 (1984a).

Population and Development Review. "Romanian population policy," 10 (1984b).

Population Investigation Committee and Royal College of Obstetricians and Gynaecologists. *Maternity in Great Britain.* London: Oxford Univ. Press, 1948.

Porch, D. *The March to the Marne.* Cambridge: Cambridge Univ. Press, 1981.

Pressat, R. "La Population de l'URSS; données récentes." *Population* 26 (July–Oct. 1972).

Preston, S. H. *Mortality Patterns in National Populations.* New York: Academic Press, 1978.

Preston, S. H. "Children and the elderly in the U.S." *Scientific American* 251, 6 (Dec. 1984).

Preston, S. H., Keyfitz, N., and Schoen, S. *Causes of Death: Life Tables for National Populations.* New York: Seminar Press, 1972.

Priagent (ed.). *Renouveau des idées sur la famille.* Paris: Institut National D'Études Démographiques, 1954.

Ramcharan, S., Pellegrin, F. A., Ray, R., and Hsu, J.-P. *The Walnut Creek Contraceptive Drug Study: A Prospective Study of the Side Effects of Oral Contraceptives,* vol. 3. Bethesda, Md.: National Institutes of Health, 1981.

Reinders, R. C. "Racialism on the Rhine: E. D. Morel and the "Black Horror on the Rhine." *International Review of Social History* 20 (1968).

Rentoul, R. *Race Culture or Race Suicide?* London: Walter Scott Publishing Co., 1906.

Richet, C. "L'Accroissement de la population française." *Revue des Deux Mondes* 51 (1882).

Riley, D. *The War in the Nursery.* London: Virago, 1983.

Roberts, J. M. *The Paris Commune from the Right.* London: Longmen, 1973.

Ryder, N. B. "Fertility trends." In J. A. Ross (ed.), *International Encyclopedia of Population,* vol. 1. New York: Free Press, 1982.

Saleeby, C. *Parenthood and Race Culture.* London: Cassell & Co., 1909.

Saleeby C. *War and Waste.* Manchester: n.p., 1914.

Saleeby, C. *The Eugenic Prospect.* London: T. Fisher Unwin, 1921.

Sanderson, W. C. "On two schools of the economics of fertility." *Population and Development Review* 2 (1976).

Sauvy, A. *Zero Growth?* New York: Praeger, 1975.

Sauvy, A. "Population changes: Contemporary models and theories." *Research in Population Economics* 3 (1981).

Savant, C.-M. "La dépeuplement de la France." *La Revue Hebdomadaire* 2 (1909).

Schiller, F. G. S. *Social Decay and Eugenic Reform.* London: Constable, 1932.

Schlesinger, R. *The Family in the U.S.S.R.* London: Routledge & Kegan Paul, 1960.

Schneider, W. "Towards the improvement of the human race: The history of eugenics in France." *Journal of Modern History* 54 (1982).

Schooling, J. Holt. "The natural increase of three populations." *Contemporary Review* 81 (1902).

Schreiber, G. "Compte rendu de la xie assemblée de la fédération internationale des organisations eugeniques." *Revue anthropologique* 45 (1935).

Seamen, B. *The Doctor's Case against the Pill.* New York: P. H. Wyden, 1969.

Searle, G. *Eugenics and Politics in Britain 1900–1914.* Leyden: Noordhoff, 1976.

Searle, G. *The Quest for National Efficiency.* Oxford: Basil Blackwell, 1971.

Second International Exhibition of Eugenics. Baltimore, Williams & Wilkins, 1923.

REFERENCES

Sen, A. *Poverty and Famines*. Oxford: Clarendon Press, 1981.

Shapiro, A.-L. "Private rights, public interest, and professional jurisdiction: The French Public Health Law of 1902." *Bulletin of the History of Medicine* 54 (1981).

Siegel, J. S., Passell, J. S., and Robinson, J. G. "Preliminary review of existing studies of the number of illegal residents in the United States." In *Staff Reports of the Select Committee on Immigration and Refugee Policy*. Washington, D.C.: U.S. Government Printing Office, 1981.

Simon, J. L. *The Ultimate Resource*. Princeton, Princeton Univ. Press, 1981.

Solzhenitsyn, A. "Why can't the West see this is no time to smile?" *The Times* (London), 11 May 1982.

Spengler, J. J. *Facing Zero Population Growth*. Raleigh, N.C.: Duke Univ. Press, 1978.

Spengler, J. J. *France Faces Depopulation*. Raleigh, N.C.: Duke Univ. Press, 1938.

Sutherland, H. *In My Path*. London: Geoffrey Bles, 1936.

Sutherland, H. "Communists and Spain." *The Month* 183 (1947).

Sutherland, H. *Control of Life*. London: Burns Oates, 1951.

Szreter, S. "The Decline of Marital Fertility in England, c. 1870–1914." Ph.D. diss., Cambridge University, Cambridge, 1984.

Talmy, R. *Histoire du mouvement familial en France (1896–1939)*. Aubenas: Études caisses d'allocations familiales, 1962.

Taylor, J. W. "The Bishop of London and the declining birth rate." *Nineteenth Century* 59 (1906).

Teitelbaum, M. S. "Fertility effects of the abolition of legal abortion in Romania." *Population Studies* 27, 3 (1972).

Teitelbaum, M. S. "International experience with fertility at or near replacement level." In C. Westoff and R. Parke (eds.), Commission on Population Growth and the American Future, *Research Reports, Volume 1: Demographic and Social Aspects of Population*. Washington, D.C.: U.S. Government Printing Office, 1973.

Teitelbaum, M. S. "Relevance of demographic transition theory for developing countries." *Science* 178 (1975).

Teitelbaum, M. S. "Aging populations." In *Encyclopedia Britannica Yearbook 1978*, New York: 1978.

Teitelbaum, M. S. "Right versus right: Immigration and refugee policy in the United States." *Foreign Affairs* 59, 1 (1980).

Teitelbaum, M. S. *The British Fertility Decline: Demographic Transition in the Crucible of the Industrial Revolution*. Princeton, N.J.: Princeton Univ. Press, 1984.

Thomson, J. A. (ed.). *Science Today*, London: Eyre & Spottiswoode, 1934.

The Times (London). "Decay of population in France," 16 Jan. 1883.

The Times (London). "Franco-German relations," 26 Jan. 1924.

The Times (London). "French government's programme," 25 April 1924.

The Times (London). "The family in France," 16 Jan. 1939.

Titmuss, R., and Titmuss, K. *Parents Revolt*. London: Secker & Warburg, 1942.

Tomlinson, R. "The Politics of *Dénatalité* during the French Third Republic" Ph.D. diss., Cambridge University, Cambridge, 1983.

Tomlinson, R. "The disappearance of France, 1896–1940: French politics and the birth rate." *Historical Journal* 28 (1985).

Toulemont, P. P. *La providence et les châtiments de la France*. Paris, J. Albanul, 1872.

Toulemont, P. P. *Un grand mal social*. Lyon: Pitrat Aîné, 1873.

Tredgold, A. "The feeble-minded." *Contemporary Review*. 97 (1910).

U.N. Department of International Economic and Social Affairs. *Demographic Indicators of Countries: Estimates and Projections as Assessed in 1980*. New York: U.N., 1982.

U.N. Department of International Economic and Social Affairs. *World Population Prospects: Estimates and Projections as Assessed in 1982*. New York: U.N., 1985.

U.N. Fund for Population Activities. *Survey of Laws on Fertility Control*, part 2. New York: U.N., 1979.

U.N. Population Division. *World Population Prospects as Assessed in 1980*. New York: U.N., 1981.

U.N. Population Division. *International Migration Policies and Programmes: A World Survey*. New York: U.N., 1982.

U.N. Statistical Office. *Yearbook of National Account Statistics, 1980*. New York: U.N., 1980.

U.N. Statistical Office. *Demographic Yearbook 1962, 1966, 1980*. New York: U.N., 1964, 1968, 1982.

U.S. Bureau of the Census. *Current Population Report* (June, 1977).

U.S. Bureau of the Census. *Historical Statistics of the United States from Colonial Times to 1970*. Washington, D.C.: U.S. Government Printing Office, 1975.

U.S. Bureau of the Census. *International Population Reports* no. 74. Washington, D.C.: U.S. Government Printing Office, 1980.

U.S. Department of Health and Human Services, Social Security Administration. *Social Security Amendments of 1983: Summary of Provisions*. Washington, D.C.: U.S. Government Printing Office, 1983a.

U.S. Department of Health and Human Services, Social Security Administration. *Social Security Strengthened: 1983 Social Security Amendments*. Washington, D.C.: U.S. Government Printing Office, 1983b.

U.S. House of Representatives, Select Committee on Population. *Fertility and Contraception in the United States*. Washington, D.C.: U.S. Government Printing Office, 1978.

U.S. Office of Management and Budget, *The Budget of the United States Government, Fiscal Year 1980*. Washington, D.C.: U.S. Government Printing Office, 1979.

van de Walle, E. *The Female Population of France in the Nineteenth Century*. Princeton, N.J.: Princeton Univ. Press, 1974.

Vessey, M. P., McPherson, K., Lawless, M., and Yeates, D. "Neoplasia of the cervix uteri and contraception: A possible adverse effect of the pill." *Lancet* 2 (1983).

Vinovskis, M. A. "The politics of abortion in the House of Representatives in 1976." In C. E. Schneider and M. A. Vinovskis (eds.), *The Law and Politics of Abortion*. Lexington, Mass.: Lexington Books, 1980.

Vizetelly, E. *With Zola in England*. London: Chatto & Windus, 1899.

Wachter, M. "Economic effects of illegal immigration." In U.S. Departments of Justice, Labor, and State, *Papers of the Interagency Task Force on Interagency Policy*. Washington, D.C.: U.S. Government Printing Office, 1979.

Wachter, M. "The labor market and illegal immigration: The outlook for the 1980s." *Industrial and Labor Relations Review* 33, 3 (1983).

Wallach, L. "The Problem of Maternal Health in Britain during the Second World War." M.Phil thesis, Cambridge University, Cambridge, 1983.

REFERENCES

Warwick, D. P. *Bitter Pills: Population Policies and Their Implementation in Eight Developing Countries*. Cambridge: Cambridge Univ. Press, 1982.

Webb, S. "Eugenics and the poor law: The minority report." *Eugenics Review* 2 (1910).

Weber, J. A. *Grow or Die!* New Rochelle, N.Y.: Arlington House, 1977.

Westoff. C. F. "Some speculations on the future of marriage and the family." *Family Planning Perspectives* 10, 2 (March–April 1978).

Westoff, C. F. "Fertility decline in the West: Causes and prospects." *Population and Development Review* 9 (1983).

Westoff, C. F., and Jones, E. F. "Contraception and sterilization in the United States, 1965–1975." *Family Planning Perspectives* 4 (July–Aug. 1977a).

Westoff, C. F., and Jones, E. F. "The secularization of U.S. Catholic birth control practices." *Family Planning Perspectives* 5 (Sept.–Oct. 1977b).

Whetham, W. C. D. *The War and the Nation: A Study of Constructive Politics*. London: John Murray, 1917.

Whetham, W. C. D., and Whetham, C. D. *The Family and the Nation: A Study in Natural Inheritance and Social Responsibility*. London: Longmans, 1909.

Whetham, W. C. D., and Whetham, C. D. *Heredity and Society*. London, Longmans, 1912.

Winter, J. M. "Britain's 'Lost Generation' of the First World War." *Population Studies*, 31 (1977).

Winter, J. M. "The fear of population decline in Western Europe, 1870–1940." In R. W. Hiorns (ed.), *Demographic Patterns in Developed Societies*. London: Taylor and Francis, 1980.

Winter, J. M. *The Great War and the British People*. London: Macmillan, 1985; Cambridge, Mass.: Harvard Univ. Press, 1985.

Wolfe, L. "The coming baby boom." *New York Magazine*, 10 Jan. 1977.

Zola, É. *Fécondité*. Paris: E. Fasquelle, 1899; English translation, E. Vizetelly, London: Chatto and Windus, 1900.

ZPG Reports, 15, 1 (Jan.–Feb. 1983).

Index

INDEX

INDEX

INDEX

INDEX

INDEX

Solzhenitsyn, Alexander, 3
Somme, Battle of, 36
Soviet Union, see USSR
Spain, 81
Spanish Civil War, 57
Spengler, J. J., 2
Spheres of influence, U.S. and USSR,
    post–World War II, 67
Sputnik, 77
Stalin, Joseph, 18, 42
Stationary population, 130
Statistique et des Études Économiques
    (French journal), 67
Sterilization, 51, 55, 57, 64, 83
    compulsory, 55, 57, 64
    of the unfit, 51
    voluntary, popularity of, 83
Stevenson, T. H., 53
Stopes, Marie, 49
Strategic demography, 17–52
    in Britain, 30–35, 39–41
    in France, 18–30, 36–39
    in Germany, 42, 51–52
    in USSR, 42
Struthers, J., 34
Suicide, collective, 3
Sutherland, Halliday, 41, 58
Sweden, 61, 81, 84, 109, 149
Switzerland, 82
    immigration policies, 150
Synthetic cohorts, 10

T

Tadzhikistan, 99
Talmy, R., 29, 30
Tavistock Institute, 76
Tawney, R. H., 59, 60
Taxes, increases, 116
Taylor, J. W., 48
Technological innovation, and age struc-
    ture, 106
Teenage pregnancy, 84
Teitelbaum, M. S., 16, 102, 109, 111
Third Reich, 125

Third Republic, France, 18, 28, 38
    decadence, 38
Times (London), 19
Titmuss, K., 59, 60
Titmuss, R., 59, 60
Total fertility rate, 6, 10
Toulemont, Pierre, 18, 19
Training, in-service, 151
Treaty of Versailles, see Versailles, Treaty
    of
Tredgold, A., 54
Tunisia, 78
    annexation, 19
Turkey, immigration to Western Europe,
    92

U

U.N., see United Nations
Underclass, 33
Unemployment, and age structure, 106
    minority youth, 107
United Kingdom, 109, 141, 144–146, 149
    immigration policies, 141
    population projections, 144–146
United Nations, 65, 88–89, 91, 94, 96, 108,
    143
    Fund for Population Activities, 94
    International Conference on
        Population, 96
    Population Division, 89, 91, 143
    Statistical Office, 88, 108
United States, 14, 68, 81–82, 91, 110–111,
    141, 144–146, 149–150
    Bureau of the Census, 68, 82
    House of Representatives, 82
    illegal immigration, 91
    immigration policies, 141, 149–150
    Office of Management and Budget, 110
    population projections, 111, 144–146
Urban poverty, 33
U.S., see United States
USSR, 18, 82, 98–100, 115–116, 135, 140
    apparent increases in mortality, 100
    Central Asian Republics, fertility, 82,
        99, 135

200